# EUROWHITENESS

HANS KUNDNANI

# Eurowhiteness

*Culture, Empire and Race
in the European Project*

HURST & COMPANY, LONDON

First published in the United Kingdom in 2023 by
C. Hurst & Co. (Publishers) Ltd.,
New Wing, Somerset House, Strand, London, WC2R 1LA
© Hans Kundnani, 2023
All rights reserved.

Distributed in the United States, Canada and Latin America by
Oxford University Press, 198 Madison Avenue, New York, NY 10016,
United States of America.

The right of Hans Kundnani to be identified as the author of
this publication is asserted by him in accordance with the
Copyright, Designs and Patents Act, 1988.

A Cataloguing-in-Publication data record for this book
is available from the British Library.

ISBN: 9781787389328

This book is printed using paper from registered sustainable
and managed sources.

www.hurstpublishers.com

# CONTENTS

# ACKNOWLEDGEMENTS

I began writing this short book while working in the Europe programme at the Royal Institute of International Affairs, better known as Chatham House. I would like to thank my colleagues in the Europe programme, with whom it was an absolute pleasure to work and from whom I learned a huge amount as we analysed European politics from London during the Brexit saga: Pepijn Bergsen, Alice Billon-Galland, Sally Nelson Said, Rudi Obasi-Adams, Tom Raines and Richard Whitman. I could not have asked for a better team with which to work for four years. I would also like to thank my counterparts Lena Khatib, James Nixey and Leslie Vinjamuri for their support during the time that I spent running the Europe programme.

I am grateful to Lola Seaton at the *New Statesman* for commissioning and editing the essay published in February 2021 from which this book emerged. After the publication of the article, several people kindly invited me to discuss the ideas in it: Fredrick Erixon at the European Centre for International Political Economy; Timothy

## ACKNOWLEDGEMENTS

Garton Ash at St. Antony's College, Oxford; Corinna Humuza at Kampnagel in Hamburg; and Mareike Kleine at the London School of Economics. Each of these discussions helped me develop the arguments in this book. I would also like to thank Robert Yates, my editor at *The Observer*, who allowed me to try out some of the ideas in this book in pieces I wrote for him.

I owe a particular debt to Peo Hansen. His own important work changed the way I thought about the early history of the European project and its relationship with European colonialism, and my conversations with him both encouraged me and helped me develop the ideas in this book. Elements of the arguments in this book were also shaped by discussions I had with Sheri Berman, Chris Bickerton, Gurminder Bhambra, Mehreen Khan, Michael Kimmage, Helen Thompson, Jon Wilson, and Jan Zielonka. I would also like to thank Anders Stephanson for his encouragement as I began to think about expanding the article in the *New Statesman* into a book.

Josie Graef and Quinn Slobodian were both of enormous help, in particular in pointing me towards academic literature of which I had been unaware. In addition to those I have already mentioned, a number of other people also read earlier drafts or chapters and gave me helpful feedback: Stefan Auer, Cemil Aydin, Sophia Besch, Megan Brown, Galip Dalay, Oliver Eberl, Noah Gordon, Keith Humphries, Anand Menon, Dirk Moses,

# ACKNOWLEDGEMENTS

Roderick Parkes, Martin Quencez, Meera Sabaratnam, Rachel Tausendfreund and Shahin Vallée. I would also like to thank József Böröcz, from whose work the title of the book is derived.

Finally I would like to thank Michael Dwyer and his team at Hurst—in particular, Anya Hutchison, who edited the text, and Daisy Leitch and Lara Weisweiller-Wu.

# INTRODUCTION

This is a rather personal book. It is written from a particular perspective—or, perhaps, from several particular perspectives at the same time. My father was Indian and my mother is Dutch, and I was born and grew up in the United Kingdom. My personal relationship with European identity and with the European Union has therefore been shaped by the influence of an upbringing in a country on the geographical periphery of Europe with a notoriously semi-detached relationship to it and, in addition to my British identity, a secondary sense of belonging to one country that is an EU member state—one of the original Six—and to another that is outside Europe and the EU but was colonised by Britain.

This has meant that although I have always felt European to some extent—in fact I may have felt more European than some British people without a parent from another EU member state—I did not feel "100 per cent European" as I have heard some other people proudly describe themselves. While the idea of being European captured part of my identity, it could never capture all of it. In particular, in addition to being European, I also saw myself as being Asian in a sense—not least because that was the usual way of categorising people in the UK with ancestors from the Indian subcontinent. Put simply, I have always had a sense of being partially, but not completely, European.

In 2009, I began working at the European Council on Foreign Relations (ECFR), a European foreign policy think tank with offices in seven European capital cities. At the time, I considered myself a "pro-European"—that is, someone who supports European integration or the "European project" in its current form. I assumed that the EU was a force for good, both internally within Europe and in the world beyond. But as I learned much more about the EU during the six years that I worked at ECFR, I began to feel that much of what I had previously thought I knew about its history was actually myth—the product of a kind of self-idealisation of the EU. At the same time as my own perceptions of the EU were changing, it was itself changing—especially after the euro crisis began in 2010. I became more critical of the EU and found it harder to continue to identify with it.

This book has emerged from these experiences. In particular, it was my sense that since 2010 there had been a troubling transformation of the EU that led me to write the book, which develops arguments that I have made in a series of shorter articles and papers during the course of the last decade. It was written in the spirit of trying to persuade Europeans that a different Europe is needed than the one we currently have—though since I am a British citizen and the UK has now left the EU, it should perhaps be "they" rather than "we". It is for the reader to decide if the perspective or perspectives from which I have written this book are clarifying or distorting and whether the experiences that have informed it have enhanced or diminished its analysis of European history and the post-war European project.

*Eurowhiteness* argues that we should think of the EU as an expression of regionalism, which we should in turn think of as being analogous to nationalism—something like nationalism but on a larger, continental scale. Just as there are different kinds of nationalism, there are different kinds of regionalism. There are different ways of thinking about these differences, but I use the distinction between ethnic/cultural and civic nationalism and apply this to regionalism. "Pro-Europeans" often imagine that the post-1945 idea of Europe is purely civic. I argue that it is more complicated: even after 1945, ethnic/cultural elements remained and found expression in the EU. However, I do not deny that there were also civic elements that were centred in particular on the social market economy and the welfare state and the depoliticised mode of governance embodied by the EU.

The influence of these civic elements of European regionalism on the European project and European identity was greatest in the period between the loss of European colonies in the 1960s and the beginning of the euro crisis in 2010. I argue that since then, and especially since the refugee crisis in 2015, this civic regionalism has given way to something much more ethnic/cultural. The deep causes of this shift, I suggest, have to do with the (neo-)liberalisation of the EU, particularly from the creation of the single market onwards, which had the effect of hollowing out the socio-economic idea of what the EU previously stood for. This left a void which was then filled by culture and ultimately produced what I call "the civilisational turn" in the European project.

The book is structured as follows. Chapter 1 discusses the idea of European regionalism. I begin by discussing the idea of a "cosmopolitan Europe" and argue that it mischaracterises the European project. I discuss the conceptual distinction between ethnic/cultural and civic nationalism and argue that we can apply it to regionalism in a similar way, and that we can also think of regions, like nations, as "imagined communities". I examine the formation of European identity and in particular the way it was defined against various non-European Others. Finally, I argue that thinking in terms of regionalism allows us to identify more clearly the dangers of a "pro-European" appropriation of far-right tropes—what I call "ethnoregionalism".

In chapter 2, I survey the long, complicated history of ideas of Europe from antiquity to World War II. In particular, I discuss the medieval idea of Europe, which was synonymous with Christianity, and the emergence in the modern period of a rationalist, racialised idea of Europe that was connected to the Enlightenment. Throughout the chapter, I emphasise some of the continuities in these ideas of Europe, in particular around the idea of a civilising mission. I argue that the post-war idea of Europe, centred on what would become the EU, did not represent as clean a break with these earlier ideas of Europe as "pro-Europeans" often imagine it did. Rather, the EU inherited some of the earlier blind spots in European thought that went back to the Enlightenment.

In chapters 3 to 5, I examine the post-war European project in three phases. Chapter 3 covers the period from 1945 to the end of the Cold War. I examine the initial period of European integration from 1945 to the early 1960s during which it was a colonial project. I show how civilisational thinking persisted after 1945 and informed the European project—in particular through the influence of western European Christian Democrats. I discuss the emergence of a new civic regionalism centred on the social market economy, the welfare state and the depoliticised mode of governance produced by European integration. Finally, I discuss the way in which, even as the Holocaust became a central collective memory in the EU, European colonialism was forgotten.

Chapter 4 covers the two decades from the end of the Cold War to 2010. I show how, during this period, there was an optimistic and perhaps hubristic mood within the EU as it enlarged to include ten new countries. It undertook what can be understood as a renewed civilising mission in central and eastern Europe. But even as the eastern borders of the EU became softer, its southern borders remained hard. Thus, although enlargement increased the diversity of the EU, it paradoxically also reinforced the sense of Europe as an exclusive space— that is, one defined by culture and religion rather than by a purely civic identity. Finally, I discuss the way in which, during this optimistic phase of the European project, the EU was imagined as "civilising" international politics itself.

In chapter 5 I discuss developments in the period from 2010 onwards. I argue that the shock of the euro crisis brought to an end the previous expansive phase of the European project and put the EU into a more defensive mode. In this context, the EU came to think of itself less as a *model* and more as a *competitor*—though whereas some thought of this in economic terms, others thought of it in geopolitical terms, and others still in civilisational terms. As further crises followed, the EU increasingly saw itself as being surrounded by threats. I argue that, in particular after the refugee crisis, the threats to the EU were perceived in cultural terms as the EU focused on defending what it called the "European Way of Life". Thus an ethnic/cultural version of European identity—what I call "Eurowhiteness"— seemed to be becoming stronger.

This short book—a long essay, really—is not meant to be a history of the EU as such, though from chapters 2 to 5 I proceed chronologically. It does not attempt to exhaustively discuss the factors involved in European integration and is meant to complement the existing literature on the EU rather than to replace it. In particular, it does not discuss in depth the institutional questions and theories of European integration on which many books about the EU focus. It does discuss the evolution of the European institutions, but only to provide context; the main focus is on questions around European collective memory and identity, the imaginary and political borders of Europe, and the evolution of ideas of European civilisation and a European "civilising mission".

The book has three aims. First, by introducing the concept of regionalism, it offers a different way of thinking about European identity and the EU and their relationship with nationalism. Second, it aims to explore the relationship between ideas of Europe and whiteness—a relationship which, given the obvious connections between the terms "European" and "white", has received surprisingly little attention. Third, it offers an interpretation of the evolution of the EU, especially during the last decade or so since the beginning of the euro crisis in 2010. In each of these cases, the book does not aim to give definitive answers—which a book of this length could not possibly do—but rather to stimulate debate.

Neither does the book offer any solutions to the complex institutional problems the EU faces and on which many discussions of the future of the EU focus. However, it does make an argument about the structural connection between the (neo-)liberalisation of the EU and the salience of cultural issues in European politics. As economic policy has been depoliticised within the EU, political contestation has shifted to issues around identity, immigration and Islam. Any solution to the EU's problems must therefore go beyond the usual one-dimensional debates about "more" or "less" Europe—that is, integration or disintegration—and focus instead on how democracy can be deepened within the EU. This, I would suggest, must in turn involve a repoliticisation of economic policy in order to reverse what I call "the civilisational turn" in the European project and to move back towards a more civic regionalism.[1]

However, these questions are for citizens of member states of the EU. As a British citizen, I instead end the book with some reflections on what my analysis of the EU tells us about how we should understand Brexit and the future of the UK. If it was the series of crises that the EU faced from 2010 onwards, and the transformation of the EU to which they led, that prompted the analysis in the earlier chapters of the book, the analysis in chapter 6 was prompted by the debate about Brexit following the vote by the British people to leave the EU in June 2016. Brexit—and in particular the idea of "Global Britain" which some of its advocates promoted—was seen by many in both Britain and the rest of Europe as an expression of a neo-colonial aspiration. This seemed to me to be too simple.

In particular, this simplistic interpretation of Brexit seemed to me to be a function of a disconnect between debates about Europe and debates about empire and race. In the UK, there had for decades been extensive debates about empire and race, which had explored in depth the afterlives of colonialism and its implications for race relations in the UK.[2] But although these debates were more developed than in other European countries, they were somewhat disconnected both from the story of the UK's post-war Europeanisation and from the parallel stories of empire and race in other western European countries. Conversely, debates about Europe, both in Britain and on the continent, seemed to be disconnected from issues around empire and race.

I was well aware of the history and ongoing reality of racism in Britain—not least because my first job after leaving university in the mid-1990s was at the Commission for Racial Equality, a British quango which enforced laws on racial discrimination and sought to promote racial equality in the UK.[3] But it had always seemed to me that the UK was far ahead of other European countries in terms of addressing racism. Yet in the aftermath of the Brexit vote, the UK suddenly seemed to be seen by many as the most racist country in Europe in a way that puzzled me. In reality, the relationship between Brexit and race seemed to me to be much more complicated. In particular, it was clear that Britain's ethnic minority population identified even less with Europe than its white population did.

This in turn seemed to be linked to the way in which, since the 1960s, British immigration policy had made it harder for people from Britain's former colonies to settle in the UK while making it easier for people from Europe to do so. As someone with one parent from a Commonwealth country and the other from an EU member state, this was again quite personal for me. When my parents both arrived in the UK in the 1960s, my father was in some ways less of an outsider than my mother was—for example he was able to vote whereas she was not. But during my lifetime, this has changed as non-white Commonwealth citizens have been reimagined as immigrants and the rights of Europeans have been expanded as the UK became part of the "European community".

My argument about the UK in chapter 6 follows from the analysis of the evolution of the EU and in particular of the evolution of the EU as a "community of memory" in chapter 3. In that chapter, I argue that by the end of the Cold War, the EU had become a vehicle for imperial amnesia. If that is correct, it provides a way to think in a different way about the meaning of Brexit—or at least to be able to imagine different versions of it. In particular, I argue that leaving the EU can be an opportunity for the UK to deepen both its engagement with its colonial past and its relationships with its former colonies. Although in the referendum in 2016 I voted to remain in the EU, I argue that Brexit is a chance for the UK to become less Eurocentric.

As with the argument that I make about the EU in the earlier chapters of the book, the argument about the UK in chapter 6 is not meant to be either definitive or exhaustive. I do not discuss any of the complex institutional questions around the relationship between the EU and the UK or any of the economic and security implications of Brexit on which much discussion has focused during the seven years since the referendum. Rather, I focus on what seems to me to be a misunderstood aspect of Brexit—that is, the role of questions of empire and race within it—in order to add further complexity to what is already a very complex story. In doing so, I aim to offer alternative ways to think about possible futures for the UK outside the EU—particularly for the British left.

# 1

## EUROPEAN REGIONALISM

Many "pro-Europeans"—that is, supporters of European integration or the "European project" in its current form—imagine that the European Union is an expression of cosmopolitanism. They think it stands for diversity, inclusion and openness. It opposes nationalism and racism. It is about people "coming together" and peacefully co-operating. It is a shining example of how enemies can become partners and how diversity can be reconciled with unity. As the European Commission president José Manuel Barroso put it when the EU was awarded the Nobel Peace Prize in 2012, the European project has shown "that it is possible for peoples and nations to come together across borders" and "that it is possible to overcome the differences between 'them' and 'us.'"[1]

However, there is something rather Eurocentric in thinking of the EU in this way. In particular, by generalising about "peoples and nations" in the way Barroso does, it mistakes Europe for the world. After all, in so far

13

as the European project—that is, the process of European integration since the end of World War II—has brought people and nations together, it is of course only peoples and nations *within* Europe. It was a process that began with six western European countries in the immediate post-war period and subsequently "widened" to include other northern, western and southern European countries and, after the end of the Cold War, central and eastern European countries—but has never included the rest of the world, though of course the EU has developed policies towards it.

Since Europe is not the world, European integration is not global integration—that is, integration and openness within Europe does not mean integration with and openness to the rest of the world, though "pro-Europeans" often imply that it does. The EU's "four freedoms"—that is, free movement of capital, goods, people and services—only apply within Europe. Although internal barriers to the free movement of capital, goods and people have been progressively removed during the last seventy-five years, external barriers have persisted. In particular, while many barriers to flows of capital and goods from outside the EU have been removed (though the Common Agricultural Policy limited agricultural imports from outside the EU), barriers to the movement of people have remained.

My argument in this chapter is that this tendency to mistake Europe for the world—what might be called "the Eurocentric fallacy"—has obscured our understanding of the EU and its role in the world. In particular, it has led to an idealisation of European integration as a kind of cosmopolitan project: what I call "the myth of cosmopolitan Europe". I argue that a better way to understand the EU is as an expression of regionalism, which is analogous to nationalism rather than the opposite of it as many "pro-Europeans" imagine it to be. Thinking of the EU in terms of regionalism rather than cosmopolitanism allows us to understand more clearly the tensions within the European project—especially between ethnic/cultural and civic ideas of Europe—and recent developments in the EU.

## The myth of cosmopolitan Europe

Although the EU is not a global project as such, some European thinkers such as Jürgen Habermas have argued that it can nevertheless be understood as a cosmopolitan project. Habermas argues that globalisation led to a "debordering of economy, society and culture" and ended a historical constellation which was based on the "territorial principle" and centred on the nation state—and in doing so hollowed out democracy.[2] The EU is, or at least ought to be, a way to regain the ability to regulate markets and pursue redistributive policies now that, in the context of what Habermas calls the "post-national constellation", the nation state is no longer able to do so. But the idea of a "cosmopolitan Europe" suggests that rather than "re-bordering" and re-establishing the "territorial principle" at a higher level, the EU might transcend it.

Influenced by Kant's writings on cosmopolitanism, Habermas argues that the EU can function as a kind of basis for, or step towards, the transformation of international politics into domestic politics—in other words, a precursor to a world society.[3] Many "pro-Europeans" believe that European integration has already transformed international politics *within* Europe into domestic politics. Yet the idea of a "cosmopolitan Europe" goes further, seeing a European federal republic as a "starting point for the creation of a regime of a future *Weltinnenpolitik* ('world domestic politics') based on international treaties".[4] Elsewhere, Habermas writes that the EU is "an important stage along the route towards a "politically constituted world society".[5] Thus the EU can "re-embed" liberalism not just on behalf of Europeans but for the whole of humanity with the "cosmopolitan goal of creating the conditions necessary for a global domestic policy".[6]

Habermas was making these arguments at a moment of optimism among "pro-Europeans", who, in the context of the transformation of Europe after the end of the Cold War and the enlargement of the EU to include central and eastern European countries, began to believe that the whole world could be remade in the image of the EU—a moment I examine in more depth in chapter

4. At the time of writing, however, this seems much less plausible. For example, in the first two decades after the end of the Cold War, it was still possible to believe that the removal of borders within the EU was a precursor to a borderless world. But during the last decade, and especially since the refugee crisis in 2015, the EU has come to see a hard external border as the necessary corollary of the removal of internal borders.

Another influential theorist of the idea of "cosmopolitan Europe" is the sociologist Ulrich Beck. As in Habermas's writing on cosmopolitan Europe, there is an ambiguity about whether it is the real existing EU or a possible future EU that Beck sees as "cosmopolitan". Beck says that his vision of cosmopolitan Europe is based on "the ideals and principles for which Europe in essence always stood and stands" and that the "European process of integration involved a *cosmopolitan momentum* from the beginning".[7] But although the EU "institutionalised" this idea of cosmopolitanism, it has been "deformed" by nationalism and there is therefore a need to "rethink Europe".[8] Yet he emphasises that this does not mean "reinventing Europe or reconstructing Europe" but rather going further with European integration and "completing the incomplete European project".[9]

Whereas Habermas's idea of cosmopolitan Europe is based on the optimistic idea that the EU could be a precursor of "world domestic politics", Beck sees the EU as a cosmopolitan project because it recognises difference in a non-hierarchical way.[10] A cosmopolitan Europe is thus "a *Europe of difference*, of accepted and recognized difference " (emphases in original).[11] However, it is only difference *within* Europe that the EU recognises in this way—in other words, Beck mistakes Europe for the world. This leads him to idealise the EU, claiming for example that "radical openness is a defining feature of the European project".[12] The "cosmopolitanism" of the EU seems to consist simply in its rejection of what he calls the "national self-delusion"—in other words, it is little more than a synonym for anti- or post-nationalism.[13]

It is possible to argue that while the EU is not inherently or structurally a cosmopolitan project, it does nevertheless have objectives or policies that can be understood as cosmopolitan. Some observers point, for example, to European approaches to development aid or the rejection by Europeans of the death penalty.[14] Another version of this argument centres on policies aimed at producing redistributive justice on a global level. But it is not clear how such objectives and policies differentiate the EU from nation states, either within Europe or beyond it, which can and do also have cosmopolitan objectives or policies in the same sense.[15] Indeed, some of the policies that are seen as examples of the EU's cosmopolitanism, such as development aid, are policies of EU member states as much as the EU itself.

Another reason why some see the EU as cosmopolitan is the set of universal values on which it is supposed to be based. Thus some "pro-Europeans" suggest that what makes the EU a distinctively cosmopolitan project is not so much its globalism as its *universalism*. In this respect, however, it is again difficult to see how this differentiates the EU from many nation states, particularly France and the United States, which also understand themselves as being based on universal values and can therefore reconcile cosmopolitanism with nationalism. Thus, in seeing Europe as an expression of cosmopolitanism—however this is defined—"pro-Europeans" exaggerate the contrast between the EU and nation states and, in doing so, idealise the European project as if it stood for the opposite of nationalism.

## Civic and ethnic/cultural regionalism

Instead of thinking of the EU as an expression of cosmopolitanism, it is more accurate and helpful to think of it as an expression of *regionalism*.[16] Regionalism is not the opposite of nationalism, as many "pro-Europeans" think of it, but rather is *analogous* to it—in other words, similar to nationalism but on a larger, continental scale.[17] That European identity is closer to national identities than to the idea of cosmopolitanism can be seen clearly by thinking about what it means to say "I am European". When you do so, you are not saying that you are a citizen of the world—let alone a "citizen of nowhere", as British prime minister Theresa May implied in a speech at the

Conservative Party conference in 2016. Rather, you are saying that you are a citizen of a particular region—and one that has a particular history and relationship with the rest of the world.

Thus, although "pro-Europeans" tend to think of European identity as being inclusive, it is in another sense *exclusive*. It is internally inclusive; it is able to include multiple European national identities and in that sense becomes more inclusive than they are. This is why people whose families cross national boundaries within Europe—whether they have lived in multiple European countries, have parents from multiple European countries, or have a partner who is from another European country—are often most attracted to the idea of thinking of themselves as being European. At the same time, however, European identity is externally exclusive—that is, it excludes those who are not European or cannot think of themselves as being European.

Thinking of European identity as a kind of regionalism allows us to think more clearly about its different versions through history. In particular, it allows us to make a conceptual distinction between civic regionalism and ethnic/cultural regionalism analogous to the distinction between civic nationalism and ethnic nationalism originally made by Hans Kohn in an influential early study of nationalism.[18] Kohn understood civic nationalism as an inclusive nationalism based on the voluntary commitment of a group of people to liberal principles as the basis for a shared sense of citizenship—in other words a political community that, at least in theory, anyone could join. Ethnic nationalism, on the other hand, was a more exclusive form of nationalism based on a shared ethnicity, language or religion.

One concrete expression of nationalism is the kind of citizenship that embodies it. Civic nationalism is generally associated with the idea of citizenship by birth: *jus soli*. Ethnic nationalism, meanwhile, is generally associated with the idea of citizenship by blood: *jus sanguinis*. *Jus soli* is generally to be found in settler societies such as the United States and other states in the Americas, while *jus sanguinis* tends to be the norm elsewhere in the world, including in Europe. (Most European countries have now converged on a model that mixes the two forms of citizenship. For example, German citizenship was traditionally based on *jus sanguinis* but was reformed in 2000 to include elements of *jus soli*. Conversely, British citizenship law was traditionally based on *jus soli* but was reformed in 1981 to include elements of *jus sanguinis*.)

Kohn associated civic nationalism with "Western" forms of nationalism and ethnic nationalism, which he saw as opposed to "liberal" nationalism, with "Eastern" forms of nationalism.[19] Kohn traces the origins of the "liberal" or Western form of nationalism from ancient Greek and Jewish thought, through the Glorious Revolution in sixteenth-century England, to the American and French revolutions, which produced the purest forms of civic nationalism. The illiberal form of nationalism that Kohn calls "organic" (that is, it understands the nation as being natural rather than willed) emerged as a response to this liberal nationalism. The paradigmatic case is the romantic version of German nationalism that emerged in opposition to French occupation during the Napoleonic era and culminated in Nazism.

In reality, however, American, British, French and German nationalisms all have both civic and ethnic/cultural elements. All forms of nationalism are to some extent exclusive; they cannot be open to the entire population of the world. Often, the differences between them are less about the degree to which they exclude others and more about whom exactly they exclude and on what basis— they can be inclusive towards some and exclusive towards others. Moreover, almost all forms of nationalism, even those that are seen as paradigmatic examples of civic nationalism, define themselves at least to some extent in ethnic/cultural terms. Thus, civic and ethnic/cultural forms of nationalism should be understood as ideal types rather than descriptions of particular national cases.

A good example of this complexity is American nationalism, which Kohn idealises as an "almost purely civic nationalism".[20] The principle of birthright citizenship, which is enshrined in the Constitution, sets the United States apart from European countries that generally made access to citizenship dependent on ethnicity, culture or religion. However, birthright citizenship was only included in the Constitution through the Fourteenth Amendment as part of what Eric Foner calls the "second founding" of the United States after the end of the American Civil War—and though it was "a dramatic repudiation of the powerful tradition of equating citizenship with whiteness", it still did not guarantee full citizenship rights for African-Americans, who were not able to vote in the South until the mid-1960s.[21] In other words, Kohn ignores the ethnic/cultural elements of American nationalism.

Nonetheless, if one puts aside Kohn's association of civic nationalism with the West and ethnic nationalism with the East, it remains a helpful conceptual distinction. It is particularly helpful in understanding European nationalisms more precisely. But rather than thinking in terms of specific national identities as being either straightforwardly civic or straightforwardly ethnic/cultural, it is more useful to think of each nationalism as having intertwined civic and ethnic/cultural elements, albeit in varying proportions, as Craig Calhoun puts it.[22] Therefore, instead of locating individual nationalisms as being on one side or the other of Kohn's dichotomy, it is more useful to study the tensions between the two sides in each case.[23]

We can also take a similar approach to European regionalism. In the long, complex history of the idea of Europe, it has had both civic and ethnic/cultural elements, as I will show in the remaining chapters of this book. Like national identities in Europe, modern European identity emerged out of the Enlightenment, producing a racialised, rationalist identity which included both ethnic/cultural and civic elements. After World War II, a new, more civic identity emerged, at least among elites, that was centred on what was to become the EU. But as these elites sought to give the European project legitimacy and pathos, they constantly drew on the earlier, more ethnic/cultural version of identity—and even now, both civic and ethnic/cultural versions of European regionalism are elided.

## Europe as an imagined community

Another influential way of understanding nations, based on the work of Benedict Anderson, is as "imagined communities".[24] Nationalism functions to make nations seem "natural"—that is, as if they had always existed—but in reality they are socially constructed. Anderson argues that nationalism emerged—first in the creole societies of the Americas (that is, Brazil, the United States and the former colonies of Spain) and then in Europe—in the context of modernity and the Enlightenment. From the seventeenth century onwards, as religious certainties dissipated, monarchs lost the automatic legitimacy they had previously had, and conceptions of time changed, there was a need for a new sense of belonging to replace sacred imagined communities—that is, in the case of Europe, to replace the "imagined community of Christendom".[25]

For Anderson, the decisive factor in the emergence of nationalism was what he calls "print capitalism"—that is, the mass production and commodification of books and newspapers made possible by the printing press—which "made it possible for rapidly growing numbers of people to think about themselves, and to relate themselves to others, in profoundly new ways".[26] In particular, as the market for readers of books in Latin—which had been the lingua franca of Europe's religious elites—was quickly saturated, publishers began producing books in vernacular "national print languages", which in turn had the effect of standardising these languages. This enabled the nation to play the role of earlier religious identities in transforming contingency into meaning. "It is the magic of nations to turn chance into destiny," Anderson writes.[27]

Europe can also be understood as an "imagined community".[28] Anderson himself says that "all communities larger than primordial villages of face-to-face contact (and perhaps even these) are imagined".[29] But we can perhaps go even further. If "imagined communities" are in this sense a function of size, Europe as a region may in a sense be even more imagined than European nations. Of course, there are countries like China and India that have larger population terms than Europe as a whole, but at least compared to European nations, European regionalism is, as it were, one further step removed from a local identity. We can thus think of European regionalism as being imagined—or to put it another way, *mediated*—to an even greater extent than individual national identities in Europe.

In another sense, however, Europe may be a slightly different kind of imagined community than nations. Anderson specifies that a nation is an imagined political community that is "imagined as both inherently limited and sovereign".[30] He writes:

> The nation is imagined as *limited* because even the largest of them, encompassing perhaps a billion living human beings, has finite, if elastic boundaries, beyond which lie other nations. No nation imagines itself coterminous with mankind. The most messianic nationalists do not dream of a day when all members of the human race will join their nation in the way it was possible, in certain epochs, for, say, Christians to dream of a wholly Christian planet."[31]

Europe, on the other hand, is ambiguous about its limits in a different way than nations are. It is not only that it, too, has elastic boundaries in the same way as nations do (for example, there has always been an ambiguity about where Europe ends and Asia begins) but also that it imagines itself in a different way than nations—especially around the question of whether its boundaries are *finite*.[32]

As I have already mentioned, "pro-Europeans" have sometimes seen the EU as an expansive community that would remake the world in its own image—especially in the two decades after the end of the Cold War, as I will discuss in chapter 3. In other words, European regionalism has something of the messianic aspirations that Anderson ascribes to earlier religious identities—which may in turn have to do with the way that European identity was originally largely synonymous with Christianity, as I will discuss in chapter 2. But in recent years, the EU has become clearer about its limits. In doing so, "pro-European" thinking on sovereignty is also changing. "Pro-Europeans" had traditionally rejected the idea of sovereignty as anachronistic and saw European integration as a way to overcome it. But during the last decade, they have embraced the idea of "European sovereignty", as I will discuss in chapter 5. In other words, European regionalism may be becoming *more* like nationalism than it was previously.

At the beginning of the post-war project of European integration, some clearly saw the possibility that a European identity could be analogous to nationalism—and even replicate its worst features. Hannah Arendt, for example, was supportive of European integration, but writing in 1948 in the context of the emerging Cold War rivalry between the United States and the Soviet Union, and at a time when there was much discussion of a European federation, she observed:

> The trouble with many European intellectuals in this respect is that now the long-wished-for European federation is a definite possibility, new constellations of

27

world powers make it only too easy to apply their former nationalism to a larger structure and become as
narrowly and chauvinistically European as they were
formerly German, Italian, or French.[33]

In other words, Arendt foresaw the possibility of an ethnic or cultural version of identity centred on a united
Europe.

Few "pro-Europeans" today, on the other hand, see
European identity as being analogous to nationalism in
this way.[34] This in turn has to do with the way in which,
as the corollary of idealising European identity, they
have tended to demonise national identity in general
rather than distinguishing between ethnic/cultural and
civic versions of it. Benedict Anderson describes how
common it is for "progressive, cosmopolitan intellectuals (particularly in Europe?) to insist on the near-patho-
logical character of nationalism, its roots in fear and
hatred of the Other, and its affinities with racism".[35] The
tendency to view nationalism in this way is particularly
strong among "pro-Europeans". At best, they see it as an
anachronism. At worst, they see it as a dangerous force.
As French president François Mitterrand put it in his
last speech to the European Parliament in 1995:
"Nationalism is war."[36]

However, there is also something Eurocentric about
viewing nationalism in this way. It is difficult to square
the idea of nationalism as a "dark, elemental, unpredict-
able force of primordial nature, threatening the orderly

calm of civilized life", as Partha Chatterjee puts it, with the experience of anti-colonial nationalism such as that in India at the time of its independence struggle.[37] Seeing nationalism in purely negative terms obscures what Chatterjee calls its "emancipatory aspects".[38] By exaggerating the differences between nationalism and regionalism, Europeans—and especially Germans, who tend to see the history of the nation state through the prism of their own experience with it—have also created a blind spot around the possibility that European regionalism could resemble European nationalisms.

A good example of this blind spot is the way in which the EU responded to the COVID-19 pandemic in 2020. At the beginning of March, as the virus swept through Europe, with Italy hit particularly badly, France and Germany imposed restrictions on the export of personal protective equipment (PPE). This was generally seen by "pro-Europeans" as dangerous nationalism.[39] A week later, when these restrictions were lifted and the EU itself restricted the export of PPE beyond Europe, it was seen as a triumph of European unity.[40] "We need to help each other," European Commission president Ursula von der Leyen said.[41] But there seemed to be little awareness among "pro-Europeans" that the EU had done precisely what they had criticised member states for, except at a regional level—and with potentially even worse consequences for the world.

Similarly, when Germany took over the six-month presidency of the EU in 2020, it chose the slogan "Making

Europe strong again together". The German government had therefore adopted the Trump administration's slogan of "Make America Great Again" but, because it now applied to a region rather than a nation, imagined that this would transform its meaning into the opposite of that signified by Trump. Wolfgang Ischinger, a former German diplomat and passionate "pro-European", could not see the problem with the slogan. "Germany advocating a strong EU is the exact opposite of promoting or glorifying nationalism", he tweeted.[42] In other words, far-right tropes were apparently not a problem, or magically ceased to be far-right tropes when adopted by Europe as a region rather than by nation states.

## *Identity formation and constitutive outsiders*

In order to go further in understanding the similarities and differences between European nationalisms and European regionalism—and thus to think about exactly what kind of imagined community Europe is—it is necessary is to examine in more detail the process of identity formation in each case. But in doing so it is important to distinguish myths about national and regional identities—that is, simplifying and comforting stories that are themselves the product of nationalism or regionalism—from more critical accounts of identity formation. Because "pro-Europeans" themselves believe in the importance of strengthening European identity, their attempts to create a "narrative" for the EU often mythologise it in order to create a "useable past" rather than deepen our understanding of it.[43]

In particular, there is a tendency to think of European identity formation based on an idealised and simplistic view of its history. Europe is often imagined as a closed system—in other words, as a region that has its own self-contained history separate from that of other regions. This reduces European history to a linear story, going from ancient Greece and Rome through Christianity, the Renaissance, the Enlightenment and finally to the EU. It erases the deep interconnections with other histories—both the multiple external influences on Europe, particularly from Africa and the Middle East (that is, the presence of non-Europe within Europe) and the interactions of Europeans with the rest of the world beyond the contested and shifting geographical boundaries of Europe (that is, the presence of Europe within non-Europe).[44]

In terms of identity formation, thinking of Europe as a closed system in this way obscures the role of "constitutive outsiders"—that is, the Others against whom an identity is defined. Stuart Hall writes that identities are "constructed through difference: they are what they are because of all the things they are not, because of what they lack."[45] This is especially true for Europe, which "has constantly, at different times, in different ways, and in relation to different 'others', tried to establish what it is—its identity—by symbolically marking its difference from 'them.'" European identity and the wider idea of the West were shaped "not just by the internal processes that gradually moulded western European countries into a distinct form of society, but also through Europe's sense of difference from other worlds—how it came to represent itself in relation to these others."[46]

In this sense, European identity was formed in a similar way to national identities in Europe—that is, against Others. Yet national identities in Europe were defined to a large extent in opposition to *each other*. In other words, their Others were other Europeans. For example, Britishness was from the eighteenth century onwards defined in opposition to external enemies, and above all France. "The overwhelming Catholicism of large parts of continental Europe, and especially of France and Spain, provided a newly invented Britain with a formidable 'other', against which it could usefully define itself," Linda Colley writes.[47] Similarly, from the nineteenth century onwards, German nationalism was also defined against France.[48] After 1848 especially, German identity was defined in terms of an idea of German *Kultur* that was contrasted with French *Zivilisation*.

In contrast, European identity formed in opposition to multiple non-European Others, the relative importance of which changed over time, as I will show in chapter 2. During the medieval period, when Europe was largely synonymous with Christianity, Jews were its primary internal Other and Islam was its primary external

Other. From the Enlightenment onwards, and especially in the colonial era, non-white people around the world became Europe's "constitutive outsiders". In the twentieth century, Europe was increasingly defined against— and seen as being in competition with—Russia and the United States. As I will show, the post-war idea of Europe centred on the EU did not break with this history of Othering as cleanly as many "pro-Europeans" would like to think.

Although "pro-Europeans" do not generally see European identity as being analogous to nationalism, they do recognise that "building Europe" is analogous to the process of nation-building, especially the more self-conscious "modular" version of it in the nineteenth century. In fact, they often point to this type of nation-building in Europe as a precedent for the creation of a European *demos*. For example, Jürgen Habermas points to the way in which the European states of the nineteenth century "gradually *created* national consciousness and civic solidarity" and suggests that doing so again on a European level would be a natural evolution. "Why should this learning process not continue on, beyond national borders?" he asks.[49] Thus the similarity between nationalism and regionalism becomes a source of optimism for "pro-Europeans".

This analogy in terms of the process of identity formation notwithstanding, "pro-Europeans" nevertheless insist that European regionalism is qualitatively different and normatively superior to nationalism, as Habermas's idea of a "learning process" implies. In speaking of Europe, however, many "pro-Europeans" draw on concepts that suggest not so much a continental version of Habermas's concept of *Verfassungspatriotismus*, or "constitutional patriotism"—that is, a civic regionalism—as an ethnic/cultural regionalism. This illustrates again the tension at the centre of the way in which European identity and the EU are imagined. "Pro-Europeans" think of Europe as being different than a nation, or even its opposite, but often talk about it in very similar ways to nationalists talking about the nation.

A good example is the idea of Europe as a *Schicksalsgemeinschaft*, or "community of fate". The concept is usually seen as problematic when used in a national context, especially in Germany. In particular, it is seen as suggesting an atavistic or pre-political idea of the nation. Yet the term is often applied to the EU by "pro-Europeans", who seem to see it as entirely unproblematic when applied at the regional rather than the national level. For example, Edgar Morin wrote in 1990 that Europeans had become conscious of their common destiny since 1945 and had now "arrived at the moment of the community of fate".[50] As Europeans have felt increasingly threatened, particularly since the beginning of the war in Ukraine, it has further strengthened the sense of EU as a "community of fate".

## *Ethnoregionalism*

A final reason that it is helpful to think of the EU as the expression of a kind of regionalism that is analogous to nationalism is that it allows us to see political developments in Europe today with greater clarity—in particular, the emergence of what might be called ethnoregionalism. During the last decade, much debate about European politics has revolved around a series of aligned binary oppositions: liberalism and illiberalism; centrism and populism; and internationalism/globalism and nationalism/patriotism. That binary way of thinking has focused attention on the use of problematic tropes and policies by the Eurosceptic far right, while obscuring centre-right parties' adoption of many of the same tropes and implementation of many of the same policies, just in the name of Europe rather than the nation—in other words, something like what Hannah Arendt feared.

In the last decade, much of the debate about European politics has centred on the apparently inexorable rise of "populism". This has been generally assumed to be a national phenomenon—often so much so that nationalism and populism are conflated in concepts like "national populism". Yet this conflation of nationalism and populism simplifies the way in which far-right figures, parties and movements talk about Europe, which cannot be reduced to Euroscepticism and is in reality much more ambiguous and ambivalent.[51] In particular, far-right politicians often speak about European civilisation, which they identify with Christianity and see as being threatened, especially by immigration from Muslim countries. They therefore see themselves not just as nationalists but also as European regionalists—specifically, as the defenders of a Europe defined in ethnic/cultural rather than civic terms.

Rogers Brubaker identifies a distinct variety of national populism in northern and western European countries, which first emerged in the Netherlands. It combines far-right positions on issues like immigration and Islam with liberal positions on issues like gender equality, gay rights and freedom of speech—indeed, far-right parties in countries like the Netherlands often justify the former by reference to the latter.[52] In contrast, he argues, the far right in central and eastern European countries like Hungary and Poland has more illiberal positions on these issues. However, this may overstate the difference between a "civilisationalist" and secularist northern and western European far right and a "nationalist" and religious central and eastern European far right.

It may be more helpful to think of the far right across Europe in terms of a mixture of nationalism and civilisationalism—that is, to use Brubaker's terms, they "construe the opposition between self and other" in terms that are not only "narrowly national" but also "broadly civilisational", even if there are differences between them in terms of the emphasis placed on each of the two elements. In any case, the crucial point here is that the far right in Europe does not simply speak on behalf of the nation *against* Europe, but also *on behalf of* Europe— that is, on behalf of "a different kind of imagined community, located at a different level of cultural and political space", than the nation. In a sense, therefore, the far right is also "pro-European".

The response of mainstream "pro-European" parties to the rise of the far right has been to challenge it—and even to claim to stand for the opposite of the far right— while also adopting some of its framing and positions.[53] In particular, while rejecting the nationalism of the Eurosceptic far right, the "pro-European" centre-right has adopted its idea of a threatened European civilisation. Thus the distinction between the centre right and the far right has become increasingly blurred. Indeed, it has sometimes seemed as if the only thing that clearly differentiates the centre right from the far right in Europe is its attitude to the EU itself. In that sense, it is possible to speak of "regional populism": a "pro-European" version of "national populism".

A particularly influential far-right trope that some centre-right figures have invoked is the idea of a "great replacement". In his 2011 book *Le Grand Remplacement*, the French writer Renaud Camus argued that Muslim immigration threatened to destroy European civilisation. "White replacement theory" has influenced the far right in Europe and beyond (in particular, it influenced Brenton Tarrant, who killed fifty-one people at two mosques in Christchurch in New Zealand in 2019, and Payton Gendron, who killed ten people in a mostly African-American community in Buffalo in 2022).[54] But under pressure from the far-right Rassemblement National, other French politicians like Valerie Pécresse, the Republican candidate in the 2022 presidential election, have also begun to allude to the idea of a "great replacement".[55]

Perhaps even more worryingly, however—and harder even to see—is the more subtle way in which white replacement theory is influencing thinking about the EU itself and producing a "pro-European" version of it. Whereas nationalists emphasise the "replacement" of a particular nation or people such as France, some "pro-Europeans" have "Europeanised" this trope and worry about the "replacement" of a Europe defined in ethnic/cultural terms. Indeed, for some, the fear of replacement is precisely what should unite Europeans. This can be seen particularly in debates about immigration, which is seen as a threat to the "European Way of Life", but also in debates about the need for a European foreign policy to prevent the "disappearance" of Europe. I discuss these developments in greater depth in chapter 5.

I argue that, during the last decade, a kind of defensive civilisationalism has emerged among "pro-Europeans"—what I call the civilisational turn in the European project.[56] But the "pro-European" way in which civilisational tropes and policies have been framed has obscured how problematic they are. The reason that it has been hard even to see the creeping influence of far-right ideas on the European project is the binary thinking which implies that the EU is antithetical to racism and therefore is incompatible with or immune from it. In fact, it has made it difficult even to discuss questions of race and racism in relation to the EU except in the most superficial way—which is particularly strange given the long, intimate historic relationship between European identity and whiteness.

In this book I do not argue that European identity can be reduced to whiteness or that European regionalism is automatically ethnic/cultural. Even before 1945, ideas of Europe included both civic and ethnic/cultural elements, as we will see in chapter 2. However, I do argue that the ethnic/cultural element of European regionalism did not simply disappear after 1945, as many "pro-Europeans" like to believe. Rather, it continued in a more subtle form—and informed the post-war European project, which did not create a new, purely civic regionalism. Rather than European regionalism in general, it is this ethnic/cultural element of European regionalism, particularly the post-World War II version of it centred on the EU, that we might call "Eurowhiteness".

# 2

## IDEAS OF EUROPE

"Pro-Europeans" like to think that the EU represents a kind of clean break with the continent's dark history. In particular, of course, they see it as the embodiment of a rejection of the nationalism that produced centuries of military conflict within Europe, especially between France and Germany, and culminated in two world wars. In rejecting nationalism, however, they also imagine that they have overcome other related currents in European history, like racism. As Mark Leonard puts it: "Europe's Other is its own past."[1] While some "pro-Europeans" celebrate this break, others see it as a problem. For example, Luuk van Middelaar argues that the EU has gone so far as to "cut itself off" from Europe's pre-1945 history, which prevents its leaders from being able to tell a story about Europe in the way that their counterparts can.[2]

At the same time, however, the continent's pre-1945 history is constantly invoked as a source of inspiration and legitimacy for the EU. In particular, the EU invokes the Enlightenment, which is seen as the basis for the "European values" for which the EU stands. It also celebrates cultural, intellectual and political figures like the Renaissance humanist Erasmus, in whose name the EU funds a student exchange programme. Thus the claim that the EU has "cut itself off from its history" is too simple, and the way in which it has rejected European history is much more specific than it suggests. Rather, supporters of the EU see it as inheriting the good in European history while rejecting the bad. The EU is imagined as a kind of distillation of what is good in European history—or the product of its lessons.

However, this idealised view of European progress—a butterfly emerging from a chrysalis, as Edgar Morin imagined it—simplifies the relationship of the EU to its past.[3] There are deep continuities in the history of the idea of Europe that are too complex to be captured by the idea of a simple embrace of what is good and a rejection of what is bad. The way that the EU is imagined also draws on more disturbing elements of the history of the idea of Europe—ethnic/cultural elements as well as civic elements of European regionalism. In this chapter, I summarise the history of the idea of Europe from ancient Greece to World War II. What runs through it is a sense of superiority and a concomitant impulse to "civilise" the rest of the world, which evolved from a religious mission in the medieval period to a rationalist, racialised mission in the modern period.

## *Medieval Europe and Christianity*

The idea of Europe begins, appropriately, with myth. Europa was a Phoenician princess (that is, from present-day Lebanon) who was abducted by Zeus—disguised as a white bull—and brought to Crete. But for the ancient Greeks, the geographical region with which she thus became identified was an indeterminate one. The first reference to a space called "Europa" is in the Homeric "Hymn to Apollo" in the sixth or seventh century BCE, where it designated not Crete but mainland Greece as distinct from the Aegean islands. Herodotus was the first to discuss the space called Europe at greater length, only to conclude that its borders were "quite unknown" and that Libya [that is, Africa], Asia and Europe were "in reality one".[4] However, he was certain that Europa herself, whom he thought had probably been kidnapped not by Zeus but by the Cretans themselves, "was an Asiatic" who "had never even set foot on the land which the Greeks now call Europe".

Apart from the name itself, what Europeans inherited from the Greeks was the idea of a contrast between their own *polis*, or polity, and "barbarism", which they identified with the other two regions of the *oecumene* (the known, inhabited or habitable world), and in particular with the Persians.[5] For the Greeks and the Romans, who accepted the Greeks' tripartite division of the world into Africa, Asia and Europe, the inhabitants of much of what we now think of as Europe (for example Germans) were themselves barbarians. But Europeans would come to see others as barbarians and themselves as the inheritors of ancient Greek and Roman civilisation. Thus, even as the geographical boundaries of "Europe" shifted, the contrast between civilisation, identified with Europe, and barbarism, identified with others, remained.

It was in the medieval period that the indeterminate space of Europe began to become an *identity*. The first time that people were described as "Europeans" seems to be the reference to *europenses* in the Mozarabic Chronicle, a Latin history of the Umayyad conquest of Hispania—that is, the Iberian Peninsula—that was written anonymously and published in 754. The word appears in the context of a description of the Battle of Tours (known in France as the Battle of Poitiers) in 732, in which the Frankish leader Charles Martel defeated Umayyad forces—in particular, "Europeans" are contrasted with "Arabs".[6] This reference to "Europeans" as a people, as opposed to Europe as a space, is often seen as the beginning of European identity, though for the next several hundred years, references to "Europeans" remained rare.

To the extent that the term was used, however—in other words, to the extent that there was a European identity—it was largely synonymous with Christianity, which was defined in opposition to multiple non-Christian Others, who were in turn identified with barbarism.

Medieval anti-Semitism, centred on alleged religious practices like the blood libel, made Jews Europe's primary internal Other. Following the split between the Roman Catholic and Eastern Orthodox churches in the eleventh century, what we now think of as the European continent was also divided into eastern and western churches—which meant that Orthodoxy could also function as an Other for a Catholic western Europe. But it was above all in opposition to Islam that Europe was defined—which in turn reinforced the sense of a unified Christian Europe despite the schism.

This early European identity formation in opposition to Islam took place in the context of protracted conflict with Muslims both within and beyond Europe. Within Europe, much of the Iberian Peninsula had been ruled by Muslims since they had defeated the Visigoths in 711 and became known as Al-Andalus. But over the next 700 years, during the Reconquista, Muslim forces were gradually pushed southwards, culminating in the fall in 1492 of the Emirate of Granada, the last independent Muslim state in Europe. Beyond Europe, the Crusades from the eleventh to the thirteenth centuries helped further solidify the sense of a Christian/European identity. As Shane Weller puts it, the crusaders were, in today's terms, a "multinational" force, united by both the idea of Christendom and that of Europe.[7]

For most of this period, according to Denys Hay, Christendom was a much more resonant term than

Europe and was used much more frequently than it.[8] But across the fourteenth and especially the fifteenth century, he argues, the use and emotional content of the word Europe increased significantly. By then, most of what we now understand as western and southern Europe had been "Christianized", while the wider spread of Christianity had been halted as Muslim forces had consolidated control over what we now think of as south-eastern Europe and the Middle East, including Jerusalem itself.[9] Thus Europe and Christendom "merged".[10] But as the power of the church within western and southern Europe declined, Hay argues, a "European self-consciousness" emerged which "usurped" or "evicted" the earlier identity centred on Christianity.[11]

This sense of a Europe identified with Christianity was informed both by perception of a threat from Islam and by a proselytising mission—in other words, it had a defensive and an offensive aspect. Even as the Iberian Peninsula remained under Muslim rule, the Crusaders sought to expand Christendom. But after the end of the Crusades in 1291, and especially after the fall of Constantinople to the expanding Ottoman empire in 1453, Europeans became more defensive. For example, Pope Pius II—according to Hay, the first pope to use the adjective "European" frequently—sought to mobilise a force to defend "our Christian Europe".[12] This period, dominated by fear of Muslim advances in Europe, continued until the end of the siege of Vienna by the Ottoman

Empire in 1529. After this, the offensive mission would be revived—and in the early modern period spread to other parts of the world that Europeans discovered.

More than anyone else, the figure who embodies the medieval idea of Europe is Charles Martel's grandson Charlemagne (747–814), who expanded the Frankish state into the Carolingian Empire, covering much of western Europe, that later evolved into the Holy Roman Empire. Charlemagne continued the Christianisation of Europe, often brutally, and, after crossing the Pyrenees in 778, played a key role in the Reconquista—a role mythologised in the eleventh-century epic poem "The Song of Roland". Because he unified at least the western half of the continent, reconnecting what are now Italy and France, he was described by contemporaries as the "father of Europe".[13] He remains a European figurehead or icon to this day: the most prestigious prize for "work done in the service of European unification" is still awarded in his name every year in Aachen, where he was buried in 814.

In Benedict Anderson's analysis, nationalism emerged at a time when religious identities were losing traction from the eighteenth century onwards. In that sense, European nationalisms can be thought of as an alternative to the earlier imagined community of Christendom. In this respect, however, European regionalism is somewhat different. As a new, more complex idea of Europe emerged in the modern period, elements of the earlier medieval version of European identity synonymous with Christianity remained embedded within it.[14] In particular, the idea of a Europe that was synonymous with Christianity and defined against Islam persisted into the modern period through the conflict between the Habsburg empire and the Ottoman empire. Thus, when the European project began after World War II, it would look for inspiration to the figure who centuries earlier had unified western Europe in the name of Christianity.

## Modern Europe and whiteness

It was in the modern period that a new, more complex idea of Europe emerged, based on the sense that it was a distinct civilisation that was more advanced or developed because it was more rational. Central to this modern idea of Europe was the scientific revolution and the Enlightenment, which created a secular, rationalist conception of identity. During the medieval period, Europeans had thought that it was their Christianity—that is, a particular set of religious beliefs—that made them distinctive. But in the modern period, some Europeans, beginning with Machiavelli, began to imagine that it was their secularism—the separation between church and state—that set them apart. European identity thus began to be understood in political terms. This can therefore be seen as the beginning of a civic European regionalism.

However, this modern European identity formation based on the Enlightenment also took place in the context of the encounter of Europeans with the populations of Africa, Asia and the Americas from the fifteenth century onwards—and is impossible to separate from it. In this context, the emerging idea of Europe was more racial than religious. In particular, the development of modern European identity coincided with the emergence of the idea of whiteness and overlapped with it to a large extent. As David Theo Goldberg puts it: "Modern Europe imagined its Europeanity as constitutively white".[15] (Of course, throughout this period, there were non-white people in Europe, but they were, in C.L.R. James's phrase, "in Europe but not of Europe".)[16]

What subsequently became known as the Age of Discovery or Exploration, leading to the European domination of the globe that lasted several centuries, began with Portuguese expeditions along the west coast of Africa in the first half of the fifteenth century, made possible by advances in naval technology and motivated by a complex mixture of economic and religious reasons. In particular, the conquest by Portugal of Ceuta in 1415 can be seen as the beginning of European colonialism in Africa (the hero of the battle, Prince Henry the Navigator, had also been a crusader) and led to further expansion in northern Africa and expeditions via the Cape of Good Hope to India and China. In 1441, the first cargo of African slaves was brought to Portugal.

In 1492, the same year as the end of Muslim rule in Europe, Christopher Columbus arrived in what is now the Bahamas. During what Fernand Braudel called the "long sixteenth century" (that is, from 1492 to 1607, when the first permanent English settler colony in North America was established at Jamestown in Virginia), Europeans, led by Spain, established their presence in the "New World". "Discovery" and "exploration" became conquest and colonisation. Yet, at this time, Europeans still saw the differences between them and the indigenous populations of the Americas in terms that were more religious than racial—the early accounts of Columbus's voyages refer to the settlers as "the Christians".[17] Over the next several centuries, however, the racial would take up the narrativising, self-identifying work previously played by the religious, as Goldberg puts it.

The shift from a more religious conception of European identity to a more racial one took place in the context of wider shifts in European colonialism in the Americas and in particular the emergence of the Atlantic slave trade. During the seventeenth century, England and France replaced Spain as the dominant European powers in the Americas, especially in north America and the Caribbean. This in turn was linked to a shift in the economies of European colonies. The focus of Spanish colonialism in the Americas had been on the discovery and acquisition of gold. English and French colonies, on the other hand, focused on the production of coffee, cotton, sugar and tobacco, which led to an expansion in the practice of slavery in the Americas.

It was in this context that the concept of whiteness emerged. In 1619, when the first African slaves were transported to what became the United States, there were still no "white" people in North America as such— settlers and their descendants would have seen themselves either generically as Christian or European (which were still largely synonymous) or more specifically as Dutch, English, French, and so on. It was only towards the end of the seventeenth century that "white" emerged as a synonym for "European" in the Americas. Theodore Allen argues that the concept emerged specifically as a way to undermine the solidarity between indentured Europeans and enslaved Africans manifested in uprisings like Bacon's Rebellion in Virginia in 1676–77.[18]

The term "white" was used differently at different times and in different places; in particular, those whom it included and excluded varied. Nevertheless, throughout European colonies in Africa, Asia, and the Americas, it had a broadly similar function as it did within the United States: to designate people of European origin and identify them as superior—more advanced or developed, more rational, in short more "civilised" than the native populations of the other parts of the world in which they had settled—and to justify a system of differentiated privileges and rights.[19] In each case, it erased the class and national differences between people of

European origin while emphasising the differences between them and the rest of the world. Just as the concept of whiteness played a role in integrating European immigrants into American society, therefore, it also played a role in integrating Europe itself.

These differences between Europeans and others were codified in legal documents such as France's *Code Noir*, the edict regulating slavery in its colonies in the Americas. It established the principle that the children of enslaved people were themselves slaves; regulated practices for the punishment of slaves while prohibiting torture and mutilation except by royal decree; legalised manumission; and gave freed slaves the same rights as other French subjects. When it was first introduced in 1685, it referred several times to slaves as *nègres* (a term the French had taken from the Spanish, their predecessors in the Americas) but apart from that did not use racial language. It was only in the early eighteenth century, as slavery became more racialised, that the edict began to be referred to as the *Code Noir*, first informally and then formally.[20] Conversely, the term *blancs* began to be used to refer to European settlers—or "European" was simply used as an antonym of "black".

The entangled histories of the emergence of the modern idea of Europe and the concept of whiteness meant that, from the eighteenth century onwards, "European" and "white" would become largely coterminous. Especially in a colonial context, where European powers increasingly sought to differentiate between and segregate settlers, natives and slaves, the two terms were largely interchangeable. This identification of whiteness with Europe would continue in post-World War II Apartheid South Africa, where signs said either "Europeans Only" or Whites Only"—and they were clearly understood to mean the same thing. Even now, the descriptor "white" is usually applied to people who are of European origin. In other words, the connection between Europe and whiteness remains.

## Universalism in theory and practice

Today's "pro-Europeans" would be horrified at the suggestion that their idea of Europe had anything to do with whiteness. In fact, many would find the attempt to link the two baffling and outrageous. For them, the EU stands for a set of universal values—usually democracy, human rights and the rule of law—that go back to the Enlightenment. But the Enlightenment was not a separate intellectual tradition, unrelated to the history of European colonialism from which the idea of whiteness emerged. Rather, the two things went together. The colonial project was bound up with precisely the same Enlightenment thought that "pro-Europeans" claim differentiates the EU from pre-World War II versions of European identity.

In particular, while Enlightenment ideas like the "rights of man"—the antecedent of what we would today call "human rights"—were potentially universal, they emerged from a particular European context and, moreover, were put into practice in a racialised way. What Immanuel Wallerstein has called "European universalism" (as opposed to a still-to-be-developed universal or global universalism) was thus "partial and distorted" and functioned as "the rhetoric of power".[21] Rather than simply and uncritically pointing to the universal values for which Europe is supposed to stand, it is necessary to interrogate the Enlightenment's blind spots—what Paul Gilroy has called "the particularity that lurks beneath the universalist claims of the Enlightenment project".[22]

It was the belief that Europeans stood for a set of values that came out of a particular European civilisational or cultural context, but were nevertheless universal, that produced the idea of a European *mission civilisatrice*, or civilising mission. This rationalist, racialised mission was a secularised version of the religious mission that animated Europe in the medieval period. In both cases, the civilising process was seen as good for those who were to be civilised—in the medieval period because it brought them salvation, in the modern period because it modernised or developed them. The concept of a civilising mission which brought progress would become the central way in which Europeans conceived of their relationship with the rest of the world—and would continue to animate the post-World War II European project.

Yet the reality of this civilising mission was very different than the rhetoric. A good example is the Haitian revolution, which began with a slave revolt in Saint-Domingue in 1791 and culminated in the proclamation of the new state of Haiti in 1801. The colony on the island that Columbus had named Española had been ceded to France in 1697 and, with half a million slaves by the end of the eighteenth century, become the world's largest producer of coffee and sugar.[23] During the French revolution, slavery was abolished. But in 1802 Napoleon Bonaparte restored it and sought—unsuccessfully—to crush the revolution, which was more faithful to Enlightenment principles, like equality and the rights of man, than either the American or French revolutions that are often thought to embody them.

It is tempting to see such examples—or even the whole history of colonialism and slavery—as an aberration from Enlightenment ideas. Yet it was not only that the Enlightenment went hand in hand with colonialism and slavery, but also that colonisation and slavery were carried out in the name of the Enlightenment ideas. Arguments for colonisation and slavery were in some ways similar to the ways in which Aristotle and Plato had justified enslaving "barbarians"—for example that particular groups were "natural slaves" who were incapable of reason and therefore unfit for self-government.[24] But barbarians were now "savages"—and inevitably, given the centrality of the concept of light to the

Enlightenment, colonisation was also imagined in terms of bringing light to the dark places of the earth.

It is extraordinary that this also all took place despite the centrality of the concepts of freedom and slavery to political thought during the Enlightenment. By the eighteenth century, according to David Brion Davis, slavery had become "the central metaphor for all the forces that debased the human spirit".[25] At exactly that moment, however, the economic practice of slavery was expanding and intensifying to the extent that, as Susan Buck-Morss puts it, "it came to underwrite the entire economic system of the West."[26] Yet many Enlightenment philosophers either ignored or defended it. Thus, Buck-Morss writes, they "railed against slavery *except where it literally existed*".[27] Rousseau, for example, had nothing to say about the *Code Noir* which, in Haiti and in other French colonies, kept human beings in real rather than metaphorical chains.

Other Enlightenment philosophers like Immanuel Kant—the inspiration for ideas about a "cosmopolitan Europe" and for the EU's approach to international politics—went further and elaborated racial theories.[28] In "Von den verschiedenen Racen der Menschen" ("On the Different Races of Human Beings"), one of several lectures on anthropology given by Kant in Königsberg in the 1770s, he distinguished four varieties or races of the human species: the "race of the whites", the "negro race", the "Hunnic (Mongolian or Kalmuck) race", and the

"Hindu or Hindustanic race".[29] Although he believed that the differences between these races could be explained in terms of climate—an idea that went back to ancient Greece and was discussed by Montesquieu—there was a hierarchy among them. The white race—which, he wrote, "is located primarily in Europe"—was at the top of the hierarchy because of its greater capacity for reason.[30]

The idea of racial hierarchy helps us understand the Enlightenment's synthesis of particularism and universalism. Kant was a monogenist who was arguing against the prevalent idea that there were different species of human beings. But because Enlightenment thinkers defined humanity in terms of a capacity for reason, and saw humans as being at different stages of development towards rationality, they categorised non-Europeans, or non-white people, as less (than) human. It was this kind of infrahumanisation that enabled them to reconcile universal ideas like the rights of man with their belief in European superiority. The Enlightenment made universalist claims which were "in theory valid for humanity as a whole", but "humanity was to be rather restrictively defined".[31]

To make this critique of the Enlightenment is not to suggest that there was nothing of value in it or that it should be rejected altogether. There were multiple strands within the Enlightenment, and some Enlightenment philosophers like Denis Diderot did oppose colonialism and slavery.[32] Thus Kenan Malik distinguishes between moderate and radical versions of Enlightenment thought.[33] The problem is the tendency to simplistically invoke the Enlightenment without recognising its problematic aspects. Instead, it is necessary to engage with its complexities as a step towards developing a genuinely universal universalism—an approach that follows generations of thinkers, including many from the anti-imperialist and black radical traditions, who sought not to reject universalist aspirations but to realise them.

## A geopolitical Europe and the pan-European movement

In the second half of the nineteenth century, the racial theories of Enlightenment thinkers like Kant were developed into what became known as "scientific" (or "biological") racism.[34] Natural scientists in Europe and the United States went further in classifying and categorising races, establishing hierarchies between them in which Europeans were at the top; importantly, though, there were often also hierarchies among Europeans and the emergence of a new, modern form of anti-Semitism based not so much on alleged religious practices as perceptions of economic power. Influenced by Charles Darwin's theory of evolution, "social Darwinism" emerged—and with it, eugenics and ideas of "racial hygiene". In its combination of the scientific method and racism, scientific racism fused the two strands of European thought after the Enlightenment.

The emergence of scientific racism coincided with, and was used to justify, the next stage in European colonialism—the period of high imperialism. Since the beginning of the Age of Exploration, there had always been competition among European countries for colonies. In fact, European wars, for example between Britain, France and Spain, had often included conflict over colonies, for example in the Caribbean and North America. In the second half of the nineteenth century, this competition intensified as the number of "empty" spaces on earth decreased and as European powers like Belgium, Italy and Germany sought to acquire colonies of their own. But alongside competition there were also moments of co-operation between Europeans—for example at the Berlin Conference in 1884–5, which established norms and rules for the colonisation of Africa.

However, although scientific racism seemed to Europeans to prove their superiority even more conclusively than ever, they were becoming more anxious about their position in the world. For most of the modern period, Europe had been ascendant as it expanded and colonised much of the world. From the end of the nineteenth century onwards, however, there was an increasing fear that this period of European dominance or hegemony was coming to an end. In this context, Europe was also seen in geopolitical terms—in other words, as an economic and political bloc threatened by rising powers like Russia and the United States. This produced

a new defensive discourse on Europe that was reminiscent of the medieval period when Christendom was
threatened by Islam.

The anxiety about the decline of European civilisation
intensified after World War I, which further weakened
Europe relative to Russia (which had become the Soviet
Union) and the United States—and also stripped some
European countries like Germany of their colonies.
Around this time there was a spate of publications about
the decline of the West—most famously, Oswald
Spengler's 1918 book. But there was also a specific, more
narrowly European version of this anxiety, which saw
Europe as a separate civilisation from the United
States—and even as being threatened by it. The Swedish
political scientist Rudolf Kjellén, the first to use the term
"geopolitics", had already written in 1914: "We can
already witness the shadows of the American, Russian,
and Yellow perils being cast over our continent."[35]

Against this background of a sense of loss of European
power, there was much fraught discussion of the
"European spirit" among intellectuals like the French
poet Paul Valéry—often identified with a high European
culture that was threatened by mass culture. Europe
faced an intellectual as well as political crisis; the war
had shattered illusions about inevitable progress and
revealed the fragility of European civilisation. Its ability
to recover its pre-eminence would depend on a revival of
the European spirit, which had been the source of

Europe's superiority.[36] Frantz Fanon would later write in *The Wretched of the Earth*: "It is in the name of the spirit, in the name of the European spirit, that Europe has made her encroachments, that she has justified her crimes and legitimised the slavery in which she holds four-fifths of humanity."[37]

It was from this "post-catastrophic" atmosphere that the pan-European movement—the inspiration for post-war "pro-Europeanism"—emerged.[38] The movement opposed nationalism, which it saw as responsible for the war and Europe's decline, and called for a continental European federation as a way of rejuvenating the "European spirit". Yet its arguments for why Europeans must unite and overcome nationalism were based on a sense of European superiority. For example, the Spanish philosopher José Ortega y Gasset, a key figure in the movement, saw nationalism as "nothing but a mania".[39] But this was because it was diverting "European man" from his destiny to rule the world on behalf of humanity.[40] The idea was that Europe should, as Ute Frevert aptly puts it, "bury its national rivalries and resume its quest for world supremacy".[41]

This connection between calls for European unity in the aftermath of World War I and European colonialism was clear to many non-European and non-white intellectuals. For example, after the outbreak of World War I, W.E.B. Du Bois wrote a scathing essay from the perspective of the "darker peoples" of the world about the disconnect between the horror that Europeans felt about the slaughter taking place in Belgium and their apparent indifference towards, or even support for, the violence carried out by Europeans in the Belgian Congo. He asked rhetorically whether war had only become horrible now that white men were fighting white men. "To many, it is not war that alarms them, but the fact that those whites who should fight blacks are fighting each other," he wrote.[42]

In fact, a key element of the pan-European movement's vision of a united Europe was the collective exploitation and "civilisation" of Africa—an idea that became known as "Eurafrica". Members of the pan-European movement saw Africa as essential to the project of "building Europe". It would function as a source of raw materials that were essential if Europe was to compete with the British Empire, Russia and the United States, but also provide space for Europe's excess population to settle—what the German geographer Friedrich Ratzel had called *Lebensraum*. In other words, the pan-European movement proposed not so much to end European colonialism as to remove the competitive element from it. If it could be done cooperatively—a "union of all the colonizing nations" as the French general and colonial administrator Hubert Lyautey put it—it would strengthen rather than weaken Europe.[43]

The most influential figure in the pan-European movement was Richard von Coudenhove-Kalergi, the son of an Austro-Hungarian count and a Japanese woman he had met while working as a diplomat in Tokyo. In 1923, Coudenhove-Kalergi published a pamphlet called *Paneuropa*, which subsequently also became the name of the movement's journal. He saw nationalism as "the grave-digger of European civilisation".[44] But although he thought it was wrong to see European nations as separate races—and is therefore, in a typically Eurocentric way, sometimes seen as a cosmopolitan—this was not because he rejected the concept of race but because he saw Europeans collectively as a single (and superior) race.[45] A believer in the Eurafrica project, he wrote that "Europe's mission in Africa is to bring light to this darkest of continents"—a perfect illustration of how colonialism was imagined in terms of enlightenment.[46]

In 1950, Coudenhove-Kalergi would be the first recipient of the Charlemagne Prize. This award illustrates the continuities between pre- and post-war ideas of Europe. In fact, the core of "pro-European" thinking after World War II had already been established in the inter-war period—in particular, the idea that Europeans must unite in order to recover their dominant position in the world or at least prevent their further decline. After World War II, early "pro-Europeans" even took up the pan-European movement's idea of the colonial exploitation of Africa as Europe's "plantation", as we will see in chapter 3.[47] In other words, from the beginning, the European project was not just about peace, as post-war "pro-Europeans" would often later claim. It was, always, also about power.

## Europe's superiority complex

In the period from ancient Greece to the outbreak of World War II, Europe went from being an indeterminate space to an embryonic identity synonymous with Christianity or Christendom, to a more complex identity that was both rationalist and racialised, and finally, in the twentieth century, to a geopolitical bloc that needed to unite to survive. But even as the perceived content of European identity changed over time, what remained was a persistent belief in European superiority that went back to the division of the world into civilisation and barbarism that Europeans inherited from the Greeks. In other words, for as long as Europeans have thought of themselves as European, they have thought of themselves as being better than the rest of the world.

The challenge of imagining and defining the essence of this superiority was always the conspicuous cultural and religious diversity within the continent. Thus writers tended to imagine Europe through the prism of their own national cultures, which they saw as epitomising what it meant to be European; the French writer Victor Hugo saw French culture as the model for a new European culture and the German philosopher Johann Gottlieb Fichte imagined Europe as a kind of Greater

Germany.[48] (This tendency to instrumentalise the idea of Europe—which also continues today—is captured by the famous quote attributed to Bismarck: "I have always found the word 'Europe' in the mouths of those politicians who wanted from other powers something they did not dare to demand in their own name.")

Quite early on, however, some writers such as the German romantic poet Friedrich Schlegel imagined that diversity was itself distinctively European. This itself became another marker of superiority to other regions of the world, which were imagined, in a typically Eurocentric way, as being more homogenous. But it still left open the question of what, if anything, could unite Europeans. Inevitably, that unity—or identity— was constructed in opposition to an external Other. Thus, in order to reconcile internal diversity with unity, the idea of Europe had to be exclusive as well as inclusive. Over the centuries from the medieval period to the outbreak of World War II, Europe had defined itself against various external Others: from Islam to Russia and the United States.

Given this history, and especially the intimate connection between Europeanness and whiteness during the modern period, the question is how much the European identity that emerged in the post-war period and centred on the EU represented a break with it—and in particular, whether Europe really did cease to define itself against an Other except for its own past. Part of the reason it is difficult even to discuss this is the self-mythologisation of the EU. "Pro-Europeans" imagine 1945 to be a kind of *Stunde Null*, or "hour zero", from which a new Europe emerged.[49] As we have already seen in this chapter, however, the real history is messier than this myth suggests. The post-war idea of Europe was less of a clean break with pre-war ideas than "pro-Europeans" imagine it to be.

The sense of European superiority would continue in the post-World War II period. After 1945, Europeans would find new ways to imagine that they were more advanced than, or morally superior to, the rest of the world. In particular, as we will see in chapter 3, it was precisely the break they thought they had made with their past, and the lessons they believed they had learned from it, that would come to be understood as the basis of this new sense of European superiority in the post-war period. Nor did the history of Othering in European identity-formation suddenly come to an end after World War II. The European project was defined not only in opposition to Europe's past, but also in opposition to non-European Others, as we will also see in the remaining chapters of this book.

Above all, what post-war "pro-Europeans" would inherit from earlier ideas of Europe was the idea of a civilising mission—even if they did not always recognise it as such. Just as the content of the idea of Europe had changed from the medieval period to World War II, the content of Europe's civilising mission would evolve again in the post-war period—from the rationalist, racialised mission of the modern period to a much more technocratic mission in the post-war period. But "pro-Europeans" would continue to believe that Europe stood for a distinctive set of values which, although of European origin, are universal. As it had always been, the logic was, as Shane Weller puts it, that "human history is, or at least should be, the history of the Europeanization of humanity".[50]

# 3

# FROM COLONIAL PROJECT TO
# COMMUNITY OF MEMORY

The core of the conventional narrative of the EU is the idea that, after World War II, Europeans renounced war and sought to make it impossible. In 1950, French foreign minister Robert Schuman proposed pooling coal and steel production in order to make war between France and Germany "not merely unthinkable, but materially impossible".[1] The Schuman Plan, which created the European Coal and Steel Community (ECSC), is seen as the beginning of the EU as a "peace project", which, as Beck and Grande put it, "reoriented Europe's bellicose history towards the goal of reconciliation and pacification".[2] It was above all because of how the EU had contributed to the advancement of peace and reconciliation in Europe that it was awarded the Nobel Peace Prize in 2012.[3]

However, Timothy Snyder argues, this story of the creation of the EU "bears little resemblance to historical fact".[4] He points out that European countries did not reject war after 1945—and to claim that they did once again commits the Eurocentric fallacy of mistaking Europe for the world. While they rejected war within Europe, they continued fighting colonial wars outside Europe "until they lost them or were exhausted".[5] One striking illustration of this disconnect is the massacres that took place in Sétif and Guelma on 8 May 1945: the brutal suppression of a demonstration for Algerian independence on the day Europe celebrated peace. Five years later, when the Schuman Declaration was signed—the supposed beginning of the EU as a "peace project"—France was fighting a brutal colonial war in Indochina.[6]

Having debunked the idealisation of the EU as a "peace project", however, Snyder goes on to idealise it in a different way. He suggests that the real story of European integration is the way in which it allowed western European countries—which were *imperial* states rather than nation states—to overcome the loss of their colonies. "The EU is the soft landing after empire," he writes.[7] Some "pro-Europeans" go even further and see the EU not just as a post-colonial project but as an anti-colonial project. For example, Mark Leonard claims that the EU "has in its genetic make-up a rejection of colonialism."[8] But this too is ahistorical. Initially, at least, European integration was not an anti-colonial or even post-colonial project, but a colonial project.

## *The colonial origins of the EU*

Between them, the six countries that would begin the process of European integration still had significant colonies after World War II. West Germany had lost its colonial possessions after World War I and Italy had lost its territories in north and east Africa after World War II.[9] The Netherlands finally gave up its brutal war to maintain control of the Dutch East Indies in 1949.[10] France, however, continued to control Indochina and vast territories in west and central Africa, as well as Algeria (part of which was administered as a group of three *départements*) and territories in the Caribbean (also administered as *départements d'outre-mer*, or overseas *départements*), with Morocco and Tunisia as protectorates.[11] Belgium also had huge territories in west and central Africa, including the Congo, which the state had acquired from King Leopold in 1908.

Although there was a consensus in France that it could and should retain these colonies—"the African people want no liberty other than that of France", said René Pleven, the French politician best known for the failed plan to create a European Defence Community (EDC) in the 1950s—it was struggling to do so.[12] This led to a relaunch of the idea of "Eurafrica" in the immediate post-war period. Supporters of the idea, including many of the EU's "founding fathers", thought that if Europe could collectively develop and modernise Africa,

in particular through an injection of West German capital, it could also enable Europe to become a "third force"
in international politics—that is, a power that could
rival the Soviet Union and the United States.[13]

In his declaration in 1950, Schuman had said that
"with increased resources, Europe will be able to pursue
the achievement of one of its essential tasks, namely, the
development of the African continent." Some in the
French government even thought of Africa as a "dowry"
in France's metaphorical marriage with West Germany—
an image Schuman himself used in a speech two weeks
after his declaration.[14] However, France did not seek to
include its colonies (or even Algeria or the *départements
d'outre-mer*) in what became the ECSC—mainly
because of fears that to do so would undermine French
sovereignty over them. In fact, during the negotiations,
it was other European countries that sought to push
France to include its colonies—in particular Italy and
the Netherlands, both wanting access to iron ore depos-
its in French colonies in north and west Africa.[15]

France's position changed in the 1950s as it became
more anxious about its colonies—in particular, after the
loss of Indochina and the launch of the Algerian War of
Independence in 1954. In this context, Megan Brown
writes that "French authorities came to see European
integration as a means to maintain their status as an
imperial power."[16] This was particularly true in the case
of Algeria. Bringing it within the scope of European

integration was seen as a way of both legitimising *Algérie française*—a "counterstrike" against the success of the Front de Libération Nationale (National Liberation Front, FLN) in mobilising international public opinion against France—and gaining access to resources to develop Algeria; and, it was hoped, to see off demands for independence.[17]

Thus, although it had not sought to include Algeria and its other colonies in the ECSC, France did insist on including them in the next major step in European integration: the Treaty of Rome, which created the European Economic Community (and the European Atomic Energy Community, EURATOM). The driving force behind it was the Belgian foreign minister Paul-Henri Spaak, another believer in the "dream of Eurafrica".[18] After the committee he chaired recommended the creation of a common market, negotiations began in May 1956. A few months later, while they were still ongoing, the Suez Crisis "generated a new wave of Europeanism" and created additional pressure to create the common market—and to include colonial possessions in Africa in it.[19] In particular, the crisis suddenly increased the importance of Algerian oil.[20]

The West Germans generally welcomed the new French position as an economic opportunity—there were fantasies of a new Ruhr in the Saharan desert—and for some, a way to get back into the colonial game from which Germany had been excluded since 1918.[21] Italy feared competition from Algerian agricultural products and the Netherlands worried that it would be dragged into France's colonial problems.[22] But in February 1957 agreement was finally reached to include Belgian, Dutch, Italian and French colonies in the treaty as "associated territories"—with Algeria named explicitly in the treaty. When it was signed in Rome a month later, the Dutch foreign minister Joseph Luns said he hoped and believed that the treaty would allow Europe to continue her "grand and global civilising mission".[23]

As a result of the agreement to include Belgian and French colonial possessions within the Treaty of Rome, most of the territory covered by it was not in Europe at all, but in Africa. Nevertheless, though these extra-European territories were now in theory part of the common market, there were restrictions on labour migration from Belgian and French colonies, including the *départements* of Algeria—in other words the principle of freedom of movement did not apply to them. Thus Belgium and France—and the EEC—were able to have the best of both worlds. After the treaty was signed, there were further difficult negotiations about its implementation, particularly between France and Italy. For example, while France wanted to direct EEC development funding towards Algeria, Italy wanted to direct it towards its own *mezzogiorno*.

The way European integration intersected with the end of European colonialism rather than following it shows that it was not even a post-colonial project, let alone an anti-colonial project. In fact, part of the point of European integration was that it was a way for France and Belgium to consolidate their colonial possessions at a time when they were unable to maintain them on their own. Many anti-imperialists saw it as a neo-colonial project. Kwame Nkrumah went so far as to compare the Treaty of Rome to the Berlin Conference of 1884–5—as we have seen, a cooperative moment in the history of European colonialism—and said that it created "a new system of collective colonialism which will be stronger and more dangerous than the old evils we are striving to liquidate".[24]

However, the colonial origins of the EU—what we might call its original sin—have been written out of the narrative of European integration. In 1992, the British historian Alan Milward published what became an influential revisionist study of the early period of European integration, which challenged the prevalent idealistic narrative and argued that it aimed not so much to overcome the nation state but to consolidate it after World War II.[25] But the intertwining of late colonialism and early European integration requires us to revise even Milward's characterisation. The first steps in European integration were not so much the "European rescue of the nation state", but, as Brown has suggested, the European rescue of the *imperial* state.[26]

## *European civilisation and the Cold War*

Within five years of the signing of the Treaty of Rome, almost all of Africa had become independent. The Belgian Congo became independent in 1960, though Belgium continued to interfere in the new state's internal affairs and helped to depose its first democratically elected prime minister, Patrice Lumumba, a year later. In 1962, Algeria became independent after a brutal eight-year war that had ended the French Fourth Republic and brought Charles de Gaulle back to power. However, after they reluctantly relinquished their last colonies, Belgium and France both sought to forget their imperial histories—just as, after the loss of the Dutch East Indies, the Netherlands had consigned the trauma to a "national memory hole", as Tony Judt puts it.[27]

It is often said the Europe of the Six corresponded closely to the size and shape of the Carolingian empire in the ninth century.[28] But the EEC was initially a "territorial space stretching from the Baltic to the Congo" and it was only from the moment when Belgium and France lost their remaining colonies in Africa that it in effect shrank dramatically to resemble Charlemagne's Europe.[29] Little has been written about the effect of this shrinkage of the EEC on "pro-European" thinking in the decades that followed it. But historians have suggested that there was an inward turn around this time as western Europeans forgot their former colonies and began to trade more with each other. Judt writes of the "distinctly parochial vision of 'Europe'" that emerged in the 1960s after the loss of empire.[30]

As Paul Betts has shown, the language of civilisation, far from disappearing after 1945, had "reemerged as a potent metaphor to ascribe positive meaning to material and moral reconstruction after the war".[31] Even more than World War I, World War II had demonstrated the fragility of European civilisation. There were some who challenged ideas about European civilisation—notably Hannah Arendt, who argued that fascism had its roots in colonialism, and Theodor Adorno and Max Horkheimer, who showed how civilisation and barbarism went together. But Nazism was largely seen as an aberration or "lapse" from European civilisation rather than as a part of it.[32] Thus "pro-Europeans" mostly continued to believe that they spoke on behalf of a superior civilisation.

However, the imaginative and actual (re-)construction of Europe in this period was of course also shaped by the overwhelming reality of the Cold War—in particular, by the perceived threat to western Europe from the Soviet Union and the dependence of western Europe on the United States. After World War I, Europe was already economically dependent on the United States— as we have seen, many who argued for integration at that time saw it as a way for Europe to compete with both the Soviet Union and the United States. But after World War II, Europe was divided between east and west, the threat to western Europe from the Soviet Union was greater, and it was also dependent on the United States for its security in a way that it had not yet been after World War I.

The Cold War is generally, and correctly, seen as an ideological struggle. But it was also often framed in terms of the shared need to defend what was perceived as an "imperiled Christian civilisation" or, sometimes, "Judeo-Christian civilisation".[33] In his famous speech in Fulton, Missouri in 1946, Churchill had referred to the threat from Communism to "Christian civilisation". The preamble to the North Atlantic Treaty, signed in 1949, also committed its signatories to the defence of "the civilisation of their peoples". In the United States, as Michael Kimmage has shown, Western Civilisation courses in universities formed the basis for an Atlanticist foreign policy that was also often framed in religious terms.[34] Thus in the Cold War idea of the West the civilisational and the ideological were conflated.

In this Cold War context, Christianity also once again became more central to the idea of Europe. In particular, through the influence on the Christian Democrats of conservative Catholic thinkers like Jacques Maritain, who blamed the secularism of the Enlightenment for the catastrophe in Europe, this renewed sense of a Christian Europe informed the first phase of European integration.[35] Rosario Forlenza has shown how the Christian Democrat idea of Europe drew on 1920s German-

Catholic ideas of the *Abendland*, or Occident, which were in turn based on a romanticised idea of medieval, pre-Reformation Christian Europe—"philosophical baggage" that the Christian Democrats "translated into the process of integration after World War II".[36]

For Catholic, centre-right "pro-European" political leaders such as Konrad Adenauer, Alcide de Gasperi and Robert Schuman, "it was obvious that Christianity was at the core of European identity, the soul at the centre of the huge bureaucratic body being constructed by politicians," as Olivier Roy puts it.[37] In particular, they saw the formation of a western European bloc in part "as a Christian bulwark against Soviet atheism", as Betts puts it.[38] Thus they imagined the EEC as representing a Christian civilisation that was threatened from the East. In fact, the Soviet Union was often imagined as being "Asiatic"—and descriptions and images of Russians drew on tropes of barbarian invaders since the medieval era. These descriptions and images "helped to conflate the Red with the Yellow menace", as Forlenza puts it.[39]

This idea of European integration as a Christian civilisational project also explains the significance of Charlemagne in its early phase. It was not just that, after the loss of Belgian and French colonies in Africa, the territory of the EEC coincided with the Carolingian empire, but also that the European project was imagined as a continuation of it in cultural and political terms. In his speech after being awarded the Charlemagne prize in

1950, Richard Coudenhove-Kalergi described the ECSC as the beginning of a "renewal of the Empire of Charlemagne".[40] According to Jean Monnet, Charles de Gaulle also imagined European integration in terms of "giving modern economic, social, strategic, and cultural shape to the work of Charlemagne".[41]

Adenauer, the West German chancellor from 1949 to 1963, embodies the "pro-European" civilisational thinking of the time perhaps more than anyone. He regretted the loss of Germany's colonies in Africa and had been a supporter of the Eurafrica project—according to Hans-Peter Schwarz, he remained a "late-nineteenth-century colonialist" who, even during the era of decolonisation, remained "convinced of the superiority of European civilisation".[42] But he also saw Marxism and materialism more generally as a threat to "Christian civilisation" or to "Christian Europe"—a typical conflation of the ideological and civilisational.[43] (Conversely, the German Social Democrat leader Kurt Schumacher, an opponent of the ECSC, saw it as part of an attempt to create a Europe that was not just capitalist and conservative but also "clerical".)[44]

However, even as western Europe continued to depend on the United States for its security in the context of the Cold War, some "pro-Europeans" were also drawn back to the pre-World War II idea of European integration as a way of creating a counterweight to American power—especially after Suez. Adenauer is generally thought of as an Atlanticist. But he was also a strong supporter of the Anglo-French invasion and during the crisis urged the French prime minister, Guy Mollet, to press ahead with European integration in response to the betrayal by the United States. "Europe will be your revenge", he is supposed to have said.[45] This idea of European integration as revenge against the United States would continue to inform the European project and would re-emerge at various points in the future. In short, Europe still had its Others.

## *A new civic regionalism*

Although, in the context of the Cold War and decolonisation, "pro-Europeans" continued to think in civilisational terms, a new European identity centred on what became the EU also began to emerge, at least among elites, that was more civic than ethnic/cultural. This new regionalism was broadly defined in terms of capitalism and democracy—in other words in terms of economic and political freedom—in opposition to a totalitarian Soviet Union. But, more specifically, it coalesced around two distinctive "models" that had emerged in post-war western Europe—a socio-economic model based on the idea of the "social market economy" and the welfare state and a political model based on the EU's "depoliticised" mode of governance—that would gradually become what many "pro-Europeans" imagined "Europe" stood for.

The social market economy was originally a German Christian Democrat idea. The term had been coined in 1946 by Alfred Müller-Armack, later the state secretary under finance minister Ludwig Erhard in the Adenauer government, to capture a compromise between ordo-liberalism and Catholic social thought.[46] It would become widely seen as producing the West German *Wirtschaftswunder*, or economic miracle. However, although it was originally a centre-right idea, centre-left parties in Europe gradually reconciled themselves to its "market" component and, used more loosely, the concept of the social market economy gradually became a shorthand for a wider European consensus on economic policy. In 2009, the concept would be formally incorporated into the European treaties.[47]

The welfare state was a key element of the social market economy that had emerged from the post-war settlement between capital and labour. European countries had begun to develop welfare provisions even before World War II—in the case of Germany, it went back to Bismarck—but it was only in the post-war period that they created the truly comprehensive systems we now recognise as welfare states.[48] In reality, as Gøsta Esping-Andersen has shown, three different models of "welfare capitalism" co-existed in Europe: a "liberal" model (as in the UK), a "conservative-corporatist" model (as in Germany and Italy), and a "social democratic" model (as in Sweden).[49] But despite these differences, the general idea of the welfare state would come to be seen as a distinctively European innovation—the "European Social Model".

The social market economy and the welfare state had been developed by European nation states in parallel and had little to do with the EEC, though they were later appropriated by it. What became the EU's political model, on the other hand, was a function of European integration itself. Often somewhat evasively described as *sui generis*, it began with the ECSC, which depoliticised coal and steel production and created an independent authority to take decisions—in part for reasons of economic efficiency and in part to prevent war between France and Germany. Future integration would follow the model of the ECSC—both in terms of the form of integration and the rhetoric that was to justify it as part of an ongoing process of reconciliation, especially between France and Germany.

From a democratic perspective, however, this depoliticised mode of governance was highly problematic. What European integration in effect did was to take policy (particularly economic policy, after the abandonment of the EDC in 1954) out of the space of democratic contestation and create rules to govern it, which could then only be challenged in the courts. As Jan-Werner Müller has shown, this mode of governance was a version of the constrained form of democracy, based on a deep distrust of popular sovereignty and again influenced by conservative Catholic thinkers, that emerged in western European nation states after World War II, especially in West Germany.[50] This new European mode of governance would create major problems for the European project in future.

The idea of a European "model" suggests that the idea of a civilising mission had not disappeared altogether even after the end of empire—and would especially inform the EEC's approach to development. "Pro-Europeans", particularly in France, would also invoke Europe's socio-economic and political models as part of the idea of a Europe defined against the United States. In particular, "pro-Europeans" saw the social market economy and the welfare state as a more humane alternative to a more brutal American form of capitalism, and the EEC's mode of governance was seen as a more cooperative and internationalist approach than US foreign policy. Thus even this new European identity centred on a political and socio-economic model had an element of Othering. Nevertheless, it was a civic regionalism—probably the closest Europeans would come to a purely civic regionalism.

The emergence of this new civic regionalism was particularly important because of the way that the ethnic and religious composition of the population of the EEC was changing as western European countries recruited immigrants to fill gaps in their labour markets. Initially, many of these immigrants came from southern Europe.

In West Germany, for example, the first *Gastarbeiter*, or "guest workers", were from Italy. But from the early 1960s onwards, western European countries also sought labour from outside Europe—in some cases from their colonies or former colonies and in some cases from other countries like Morocco and Turkey. The effect was to dramatically increase the non-white and Muslim population of the EEC. Therefore European societies became increasingly multicultural and multiracial.

The problem was that civic regionalism was never enough. Even during the so-called *trente glorieuses* when the European socio-economic and political model seemed to be working, these European models were not enough to deliver legitimacy for the EEC.[51] As World War II receded into history and the prospect of a renewed military conflict between France and West Germany seemed less and less likely, the narrative of European integration as a peace project also became less compelling as a justification for further integration. "Pro-Europeans" were therefore always tempted to draw on earlier ideas of Europe for legitimacy and pathos— hence the tendency to speak of "Europe" rather than the EEC. Thus Europe's embryonic civic regionalism would co-exist with elements drawn from the history of its ethnic/cultural regionalism—particularly ideas around European civilisation.

One illustration of the limits of the universalism of the new civic regionalism was the EEC's relations with north African states. In 1976—fourteen years after Algeria's independence—the EEC and Algeria finally negotiated a new agreement which treated it like any other "third country" and made no mention of the fact that it had ever been part of the EEC.[52] Megan Brown argues that it was at this point that the Mediterranean became fixed as the southern border of Europe.[53] That seemed to be confirmed in 1987 when Morocco applied to join the European Communities (EC, the new term for the ECSC, the EEC, and Euratom after 1967). Its application was rejected on the simple grounds that it was not a "European state"—though it remained possible for European states to have territory beyond Europe that was part of the EC.[54]

*Meanings of Europe*

By the time Morocco applied to join the EC, it had already enlarged to include six more countries in addition to the original Six, which further complicated the meaning of the Europe embodied by it. Denmark, Ireland and the United Kingdom joined the EC in 1973, followed by Greece in 1981 and Spain and Portugal in 1986. Each of these countries had different reasons for joining the EC, saw something different in it, and brought different perspectives and ideas of Europe. For the UK, it was largely a pragmatic choice.[55] For Greece, Spain and Portugal, on the other hand, joining the EU

was part of their transition to democracy after dictator-
ship and thus "signposted the promised land of political
liberalism".[56] But Denmark, Spain, Portugal, and the UK
were also former imperial powers and brought their own
colonial legacies into the EC.

For the UK, unlike for the Six who were part of the
colonial project, Europe *was* an alternative to empire. It
had remained aloof from the first steps towards European
integration in the 1950s, "secure in its cultural, political
and economic links with the non-European world", as
Tony Judt puts it.[57] But from the 1960s onwards, as trade
with the Commonwealth declined as a proportion of
total trade and trade with European countries increased,
it became more receptive.[58] Many in the UK who
opposed accession to the EEC saw it as a betrayal of the
Commonwealth. In a televised debate at the Oxford
Union during the referendum campaign in 1975, Labour
politician Barbara Castle asked: "What kind of internationalism is it that says that henceforth this country must
give priority to a Frenchman over an Indian, a German
over an Australian, an Italian over a Malaysian?"[59]

Ireland was in a unique position as a former British
colony. Nevertheless, it shared the UK's initial scepticism
about the European project and in particular its concerns
that integration would lead to an unacceptable loss of sovereignty. For example, the Irish independence leader and
taoiseach Eamonn de Valera warned that a political federation "would mean that you had a European parliament

deciding the economic circumstances ... of our life here".[60] But Ireland's links to the UK economy meant it had little choice but to join along with the British. Denmark, which had lost its small colonies around the world but still included Greenland, also followed the UK into the EC as its increasing exports to West Germany strengthened the economic case for membership—that is, it joined for similarly pragmatic reasons.[61]

After the loss of Cuba, Puerto Rico and the Philippines in the Spanish-American war in 1898, Spain's empire had been reduced to a handful of small possessions in north Africa. When Morocco became independent in 1956, Spain surrendered its own protectorate, which consisted of a small strip in the north of the country and another small strip in the south. But it held on to what became Western Sahara until 1975, when the Franco regime finally ended with his death. Thus the end of fascism and the end of empire went together. However, Spain retained the tiny enclaves of Ceuta ("the exact site where European imperialism commenced", as Peo Hansen puts it) and Melilla on the Moroccan coast.[62] With Spain's accession to the EC in 1986—the year before Morocco was told that it could not join the EC because it was in Africa rather than Europe—the bloc also reacquired territory in Africa.

Portugal was Europe's oldest colonial power and had played a leading role in the development of the Atlantic slave trade and in colonialism in Africa. It also maintained a significant colonial presence longer than any other European power; even after the humiliating loss of Goa to India in 1961, it kept fighting what was known as the Overseas War in Angola, Guinea-Bissau and Mozambique until 1974. As in the case of the UK, its imperial history was over before it joined the EC. Unlike the UK, however, and like Spain, its imperial history was bound up with the end of fascism—the coup that brought the so-called Estado Novo, or New State, to an end went together with the end of the Overseas War in 1974. Therefore for Portugal, Europe, as embodied by the EC, was both post-fascist and post-imperial.

After the suppression of a Communist insurgency which had played a central role in the beginning of the Cold War, Greece had been ruled by centrist and centre-right parties and joined NATO in 1952. But in 1967, in the name of protecting Greece from the communist threat, a group of army colonels seized power in a coup. It was only after the junta fell in 1974 following the Turkish invasion of northern Cyprus that Greece began to make a transition back to democracy—the period known as *metapolitefsi*, or regime change. The new government, led by the centre-right New Democracy party, applied to join the EC less than a year after the fall of the colonels. Thus for Greece, too, accession in 1981 was closely identified with post-authoritarianism, though it also had the effect of importing its ongoing conflict with Turkey into the EC.

In all three countries, the transition to democracy and accession negotiations took place in parallel and were seen as mutually reinforcing. In this way, the EC came to be seen as the embodiment of "European values", in particular democracy, and as the antithesis to the values of the authoritarian regimes in Greece, Portugal and Spain. Those authoritarian regimes were seen as emerging from a particular pathology of the nation state. Thus the EC was perceived not just as an economic opportunity or necessity, as it was for the UK, but as a way of saving the nation from itself. During the debate about accession, Spanish "pro-Europeans" liked to quote Ortega y Gasset, who in 1910 had said: "Spain is the problem and Europe is the solution."

In thinking of the EC in this way, Greece, Spain and Portugal had much in common with the Six and in particular with Germany, where European integration was understood as part of its difficult process of coming to terms with the Nazi past. Influenced above all by Germany's *Erinnerungskultur*, or memory culture, it was this idea of European integration as a post-fascist project as well as a "peace project" that allowed "pro-Europeans" to believe that Europe's only Other was now its own past. But while helping to further develop a more civic European regionalism, the increasing centrality of Europe's fascist past to the narrative of the European project would also increase its Eurocentrism and in particular its tendency to see its history as a "closed system".

## *The internal and external lessons of European history*

From the 1960s onwards, the Holocaust became a central collective memory in Europe and was gradually incorporated into the narrative of the European project. This was largely driven by West Germany's engagement with the Nazi past, and with its specific responsibility for the Holocaust, which had begun in the 1960s. By the mid-1980s, Holocaust memory had become part of the Federal Republic's official culture, though it remained contested, as the so-called *Historikerstreit*, or "historians' dispute", illustrated.[63] In particular, influenced in part by the work of Theodor Adorno, German Holocaust memory centred on the idea of Auschwitz as a *Zivilisationsbruch*, or "civilisational break"—that is, a uniquely evil event which represented a radical rupture with European or human civilisation up to that point.[64]

From the 1990s onwards, West Germany's memory culture was "Europeanised", turning "the task of remembrance from a German into a European obligation", as Wulf Kansteiner puts it.[65] Steps were taken to institutionalise the memory of the Holocaust, for example through European-level funding of memorials, museums, education and research.[66] The collective memory of the Holocaust fitted neatly into the idea of European integration as a "peace project" but also expanded it. Thus, Jan-Werner Müller writes, the EU came to be seen as "an institutional edifice whose foundations contain the very lessons learned from the experience of totalitarian war, conflict and European-wide genocide".[67] Set within this wider context of World War II, the Holocaust was seen as the paradigmatic European memory, a "common European founding myth" or even "the core of European identity".[68]

The Holocaust had become so essential to European identity and the official narrative of the EU that in 2005 Tony Judt could write: "Holocaust recognition is our contemporary European entry ticket".[69] In 1825 the German poet Heinrich Heine had written that for Jews, baptism was the "European entry ticket". But at the start of the twenty-first century, according to Judt, "the pertinent European reference" was not baptism but extermination. Thus in order to become European it was necessary not to convert but rather to accept the significance of the Holocaust as part of the story of internal conflicts within Europe. "The attempt by one group of Europeans to exterminate every member of another group of Europeans, here on European soil" had become a central negative reference point.[70]

In this sense, Europe was on its way to becoming a "community of memory". But collective memory is always selective memory. As the Holocaust was commemorated within the EU, European colonialism remained forgotten.[71] This "biased salience", as Avishai Margalit has called it, was particularly striking in the case of Germany itself.[72] Although the Holocaust had become central to its identity, there was almost no discussion of Germany's colonial history beyond Europe, which had itself included a genocide—the first of the twentieth century—against the Herero and Nama in German Southwest Africa (present-day Namibia) between 1904 and 1908.[73] Privileging the Holocaust, and insisting on its uniqueness, obscured its connections with colonialism and slavery to which Hannah Arendt and others such as Aimé Césaire and W.E.B. du Bois had pointed.[74]

Although some "pro-Europeans" would claim that the EU was an inherently anti-racist project, there was never an attempt to make the memory of colonialism a central European foundational memory, and it never came to influence the EU in the way that the Holocaust did. Rather, it was assumed that, simply because of the central role that the Holocaust had come to play in the narrative of the EU, it had also rejected racism more widely. With the European rejection of racism thought to be almost self-evident, there was no need even to discuss racism against non-white people in Europe—or, for example, to collect ethnic data that might identify the extent of disadvantage and discrimination. As David Theo Goldberg puts it: "There is no racism because race was buried in the rubble of Auschwitz."[75]

A good example of the EU's memory culture is a speech given by European Commission President Romano Prodi in 2004 in which he spoke of the "dark and terrible chapters" of European history.[76] Typically, he referred entirely to acts of cruelty that took place *within* Europe, in particular the history of anti-Semitism culminating in "concentration camps, mass extermination, genocide and the unique horror of the Shoah", but he said nothing about colonialism and imperialism. He said that the EU aims to learn lessons from its history— "the European idea was based on the firm determination to make sure the Europe of the future would be different"—but again he only referred here to the history of anti-Semitism and war in Europe. Yet, he said, "racism, xenophobia and anti-Semitism are a clear violation of all the Union stands for".

Thus, the emerging official narrative of the EU was based on the internal lessons of European history, i.e. what Europeans had done to each other, but not the external lessons, i.e. what Europeans had done to rest of world—in particular colonialism. The early history of the European project as a colonial project now forgotten, "pro-Europeans" saw colonialism as a problem of nation states, not the EU—though of course the EU itself could not be said to be responsible for the Holocaust either, and yet it had become a central reference point for it. Thus Timothy Snyder's claim that the EU provided western European imperial states with a "soft landing" after empire makes it sound too positive. European integration did allow them to move on from empire, but without remembering it.

In his famous lecture "Qu'est-ce qu'une nation?" ("What is a nation?"), the French historian Ernest

Renan pointed to the crucial role of forgetting in the creation of a nation. "The essence of a nation is that all individuals have many things in common, and also that they have forgotten many things," he said.[77] If regionalism is analogous to nationalism, as I argued in chapter 1, we can apply Renan's insight about nations to regions— in other words, regions also forget, and it is through this process of forgetting that regionalism emerges. In the case of the emergence of a new European regionalism after World War II, it was empire that was forgotten. By the end of the Cold War, even as the Holocaust was becoming "the core of European identity", the EU had become a vehicle for imperial amnesia.

4

# A NEW CIVILISING MISSION

In the post-Cold War period, as the EU (as it became with the Maastricht Treaty in 1992) enlarged to include former Communist countries in central and eastern Europe, there was a new mood of optimism, or perhaps hubris, among "pro-Europeans". They began to imagine that, as the EU spread its socio-economic and political models, the whole world would be remade in its image and Europe would "run the twenty-first century".[1] After World War II, Europe had been decentred—or, in Dipesh Chakrabarty's phrase, provincialised.[2] But, after the end of the Cold War, it "recentred itself by imagining itself as the laboratory of the future", as Ivan Krastev has put it.[3] In other words, what emerged was a new, somewhat technocratic version of the old idea of Europeanising the world.

It was during the two decades after the end of the Cold War that visions of Europe as an expression of cosmopolitanism emerged. The idea that Europe was "open" and had fluid borders was strengthened by enlargement, though the way that the EU sought to integrate and reform central and eastern European countries was predicated on tropes about a "backward" eastern Europe that went back to the Enlightenment. Even as the EU opened to the east, however, it remained closed to the south. In other words, although "pro-Europeans" increasingly imagined the EU as being "open" and therefore cosmopolitan, enlargement in the post-Cold War period actually strengthened the implicitly ethnic/cultural version of European identity that might be called "Eurowhiteness".

In its immediate "neighbourhood" and beyond, "pro-Europeans" argued, the EU's new approach was quite different from its historic civilising mission, not only because it now stood for different "values" based on the lessons of its history but also because it sought to promote them in a different way. It was a "civilian" or "normative" power rather than a traditional great power. Europeans would still frequently use military power beyond Europe in the post-Cold War period—sometimes even through the EU itself. But, because of the perception of European integration (that is, *internal* integration) as a "peace project", "pro-Europeans" would nevertheless imagine "Europe" as an exceptionally peaceful power. In fact, they believed the EU was "civilising" international relations itself.

## *The (neo-)liberalisation of the EU*

The bloc that central and eastern Europeans sought to join after the end of the Cold War was quite different from the EC that the second group of six member states had joined in the 1970s and 1980s. Throughout the 1970s, European integration had stalled at the political level—though, importantly, "judicial integration" continued through the European Court of Justice, whose decisions on competition law had significant distributional consequences and increased the economic liberalism of the bloc.[4] In the mid-1980s, however, there was a relaunch of the European project around the idea of the single market, which took this shift towards economic liberalisation much further.

The single market project was closely connected to the neoliberal turn—as the central role in both developments of the British prime minister, Margaret Thatcher, illustrates. The Single European Act, signed in 1985, drove deregulation, privatisation, the reduction of subsidies, and the removal of barriers to the flow of capital, goods, people and services. The regulatory competition it produced put pressure on welfare models, while aspirations for a compensatory "social" Europe, particularly on the French left, were largely frustrated. Thus this next phase of European integration undermined part of what, in the previous phase, had been thought of as the European model. As Chris Bickerton has put it: "Closer

European integration became a way of burying the post-war compromise."[5]

The creation of the single market and the new post-Cold War context led to the next phase of European integration. The Treaty on European Union, agreed by the twelve member states of the EC in Maastricht in 1992, created the EU and with it a new concept of European citizenship. It further extended the principle of freedom of movement, which had been established in the Treaty of Rome in 1957 and gave EU citizens the right to live in any other member state. (In addition, a group of western European countries had signed the Schengen Agreement, which removed borders between them in 1995.) Finally, and perhaps most importantly for the future of the European project, the Maastricht Treaty also committed ten of the twelve member states to create a single currency.

"Pro-Europeans" had long dreamed of a single European currency—in particular, as a means of challenging the hegemony of the dollar—but France and West Germany had been unable to overcome their different visions for it. However, after the fall of the Berlin Wall, with German unification imminent, French President François Mitterrand saw it as a way to constrain a more powerful Germany and pushed Chancellor Helmut Kohl to agree to finally move ahead. In return for his agreement, the new currency was created largely on German terms, with a "hyper-independent" central bank based on the Bundesbank that was committed almost exclusively to preventing inflation, and fiscal rules that set limits on deficits and debts.[6]

The creation of the single currency on these German terms created a new institutional context for the economic divisions within Europe—in particular, between the richer north and the poorer south. In order to secure the agreement of poorer countries in Europe to the Maastricht Treaty, who rightly feared that the new fiscal rules would limit policy space and growth, there was a compensatory increase in the EU's so-called structural funds. According to Tony Judt, European Commission president Jacques Delors "all but bribed" Greece, Ireland, Spain and Portugal.[7] Meanwhile, Denmark and the UK negotiated an opt-out from economic and monetary union. However, despite the flaws in its construction perceived by many economists at the time, the euro was seen by "pro-Europeans" as a triumph when it became a reality in 1999.

As the EU was becoming more liberal in economics, it was also articulating itself in terms of the "values" it stood for. In 1973, the nine member states of the EC had made their first attempt to codify "European values" in a Declaration on European Identity, which had made reference to a "common European civilisation".[8] In 1993, with central and eastern European countries in mind, the EU formalised the basis for accession—the so-called Copenhagen criteria:

Membership requires that the candidate country has achieved stability of institutions guaranteeing democracy, the rule of law, human rights and respect for and protection of minorities, the existence of a functioning market economy as well as the capacity to cope with competitive pressure and market forces within the Union. Membership presupposes the candidate's ability to take on the obligations of membership including adherence to the aims of political, economic and monetary union.[9]

Above all, the post-Cold War moment was framed in terms of democratic transition. As we saw in the previous chapter, "pro-Europeans" had increasingly come to see the EU as post-authoritarian. Specifically, because of the way in which European integration had come to be linked to Germany and Italy's transitions to democracy after World War II and similar movements in Greece, Portugal and Spain in the 1980s, the EU saw itself as playing a key role in democratic transitions. It could now help central and eastern European countries in the same way that it helped southern European countries that were now consolidated democracies and EU member states. There was a kind of democratic triumphalism among "pro-Europeans", who thought of Europe generally, and especially the EU, as a model of democratisation from which others around the world could learn.[10]

The paradox of this phase of European integration, however, was that the renewed optimism among "pro-Europeans" coincided with an increase in popular

Euroscepticism.[11] After Maastricht there was an increasing "disconnect between rulers and ruled".[12] For several decades, there had been a "permissive consensus" that had allowed "pro-European" elites to push ahead with integration without interference from citizens.[13] But as European integration had gone further, this had come to an end and a more contested EU had emerged. Euroscepticism was in part a response by citizens to the increasing economic liberalism of the EU—what in France was called *ultralibéralisme*. Yet the structure of the EU turned opposition to particular policies into fundamental opposition to the EU as a polity—in other words, it produced Euroscepticism.[14]

Because steps in European integration often involved constitutional change, they often required referendums in order to be ratified by member states. The Maastricht Treaty had passed only narrowly in a referendum in France in 1992, but in 2001, the EU began the process of trying to create a constitution for itself. It did so in a typically elitist way through a Convention on the Future of the European Union led by former French president Valéry Giscard D'Estaing. In 2005 the constitution it drafted was rejected by voters in France and the Netherlands, demonstrating the disconnect that had emerged between elites and citizens. As European integration went further, therefore, the problems of democracy in Europe—and the particularly problematic role of the EU itself in *constraining* democracy—were becoming more apparent.

Thus the EU which central and eastern European countries sought to join after the end of the Cold War was evolving in some problematic ways. After an inward-looking period from the 1960s until the end of the Cold War, the EU was now looking outward again and thinking in terms of expansion. As it did so, however, it was also itself changing internally. It stood more for neoliberalism than the socio-economic model of the earlier phase of European integration. It also thought of itself as standing for democracy, but there was an increasing backlash against the constrained form of democracy it represented. For the countries of central and eastern Europe, joining the EU would mean not only liberalising their economies but also accepting constraints on national and popular sovereignty at the exact moment they thought they were finally recovering them.

## Not yet Europe

As Larry Wolff has shown, the idea of eastern Europe as a space distinct from western Europe goes back to the Enlightenment.[15] Up to and including the Renaissance, the fundamental conceptual division of Europe had been between north and south. Europe tended to be imagined from the south—in particular, Italy, the centre of European civilisation—which looked with condescension at the barbaric north. But during the Enlightenment a "conceptual reorientation" took place as a new divide emerged between western Europe, which had replaced southern Europe as the centre of civilisation, and eastern Europe including Russia.[16] Enlightenment philosophers like Voltaire and Rousseau gazed "from west to east, instead of from south to north", as Wolff puts it.

As this reorientation took place, Eastern Europe was constructed as "a paradox of simultaneous inclusion and exclusion"—it was "Europe but not Europe".[17] In the context of the Enlightenment idea of progress, it was seen not just as barbaric but specifically as "backward"— that is, behind western Europe in developmental terms. In this sense, there is a parallel between western European perceptions of eastern Europe and the world beyond Europe; travellers described eastern Europeans as barbarians like the inhabitants of the New World.[18] Still, eastern Europe was not perceived as being quite as backward as Africa or Asia. Rather, it was an in-between space that "mediated between the poles of civilisation and barbarism".[19] In other words, unlike the non-white world, it had the potential to become European—one might say it was not yet Europe.

The end of the Cold War suddenly and dramatically changed the political geography of Europe. The continent was no longer divided simply between east and west. In particular, there was a revival of the idea of a distinctive space called central Europe—a category that had disappeared during the Cold War. But mental maps based on the idea of a "backward" eastern Europe remained, at least in western Europe, and the idea of eastern Europe as not-yet-Europe would influence the way in which the EU approached the accession of central and eastern European countries. It was seen as possible and even natural for them to join the EU and become European. First, however, they would have to be civilised.

The EU's approach to central and eastern Europe after the end of the Cold War was based on the idea of conditionality. Accession would be tied to economic, legal and political reforms based on the Copenhagen criteria that applicant countries would have to undertake to make them compatible with "European values". In practice, this meant adopting the almost 100,000 pages of rules known as the *acquis communautaire*. The process was framed in terms of democratic transition, but it also meant economic liberalisation—the privatisation of state-owned assets, liberalisation of the financial system, and reduction of government spending and subsidies. In reality, it was as much neoliberalism as good governance that the EU sought to export in central and eastern Europe.[20]

Moreover, although the process was framed in terms of supporting the transition to democracy, it had some problematic consequences from a democratic perspective that would later come back to haunt the EU. As Ivan Krastev puts it, the accession process "virtually institutionalized elite hegemony over the democratic process" while sidelining parliaments, which after the revolutions had been seen by citizens as the real representatives of the people.[21] Policy, especially economic policy, was determined by the EU's demands rather than the needs of citizens. The accession countries were even required to commit to join the euro and thus to adhere to the EU's fiscal rules. Thus citizens "experienced transitional democracies as regimes where voters could change governments but not policies."[22]

Jan Zielonka has argued that that EU can be understood as a kind of empire and its post-Cold War project of reforming and integrating its "neighbourhood" as a kind of "post-modern" civilising mission.[23] Few "pro-Europeans" imagine the EU to be an empire and most would be outraged at the suggestion that it might be, even if it has the "dimensions" of one, as former European Commission President José Manuel Barroso put it.[24] But in some respects, Zielonka argues, the EU also acts like an empire—that is, it "exercises control over diverse peripheral actors through formal annexation and/or various forms of informal domination".[25] In other words, it is not only that it has "imperial dimensions", as Barroso acknowledged, but also that it has "imperial characteristics".[26]

The EU's approach to central and eastern Europe was framed in terms of "norms" based on European values that were in turn seen as being based on the universalist ideas of the Enlightenment—and it is this, "pro-Europeans" argue, that makes it different from earlier European civilising missions. But, as Zielonka points out, imperial civilising missions were also carried out in the name of the universalist ideas of the Enlightenment. They were framed in terms of the development of colonies—in particular to make them fit for self-government. In short, they were normative as well as coercive. Even if elites in central and eastern European countries voluntarily agreed to make the reforms they were required to make, the EU's approach was nevertheless permeated by assumptions about a dominant western Europe and an inferior eastern Europe.[27]

The negotiations between the EU and eight central and eastern European countries (the Czech Republic, Estonia, Hungary, Latvia, Lithuania, Poland, Slovakia and Slovenia), along with Cyprus and Malta, went on for five years. It was in some ways a humiliating experience for the applicant countries.[28] Fearing a massive influx of immigrants from central and eastern Europe, all of the existing fifteen member states except Ireland, Sweden and the UK insisted on transitional limits—in other words a temporary restriction on the principle of freedom of movement that had been extended at Maastricht. EU subsidies were also limited. Nevertheless, all ten countries that had begun negotiations in 1998 joined the EU in 2004, making it a bloc of twenty-five member states including countries whose territory stretched into the former Soviet Union.

## The soft east and the hard south

However, while the EU's borders to the east softened in the 1990s and 2000s as it enlarged to include central and eastern European countries, its borders to the south remained hard. As we saw in chapter 3, Morocco's application to join the EEC in 1987 was rejected on the simple grounds that it was not part of Europe in geographic terms—even though, as a group of three French *départements*, part of Algeria had been part of the EEC for five years from the Treaty of Rome in 1957 to its independence in 1962. The inclusion of central and eastern European countries played a key part in strengthening the sense among many "pro-Europeans" that the EU was radically "open". But as far as north Africa and the Middle East were concerned, it remained very much closed.

EU officials insisted that its borders were defined by values rather than geography. "Geography sets the frame, but fundamentally it is values that make the borders of Europe," wrote Olli Rehn, the EU's commissioner for enlargement, in 2005 following the "big bang" enlargement of the previous year, with Bulgaria and Romania set to join by 2007 and some now thinking about the prospect of a next phase of enlargement to include the western Balkans.[29] Enlargement was "a matter of extending the zone of European values, the most fundamental of which are liberty and solidarity, tolerance and human rights, democracy and the rule of law." In other words, the EU conceived of itself in normative terms—and even if geography set parameters, this had nothing to do with an ethnic/cultural idea of European identity.

The reality, however, was somewhat different. For the same reasons that had been given to Morocco in 1987—

that it was simply not part of Europe in geographic terms—there was never any question of north African or middle eastern countries joining the EU, however aligned they were with the EU's values. Instead, the EU developed a series of initiatives to deal with them: the Euro-Mediterranean Partnership (created in 1995), the European Neighbourhood Policy (created in 2003), and the Union for the Mediterranean (created in 2008). Through these various vehicles, the EU sought to put pressure on north African and middle eastern countries to carry out economic and political reforms along the lines of those implemented in eastern Europe—but without the prospect of membership even if they were to complete them.

Moreover, the EU's rhetoric about its openness and the normative way in which it understood its borders, and about its aspiration to "extend its zone of values", obscured its other unstated interest in north Africa: to prevent migration flows. Thus, though it claimed to be encouraging states like Algeria and Egypt to develop good governance, the reality was somewhat different. The EU itself, and individual member states like France and Italy, maintained cosy relationships with autocratic rulers like Tunisian President Zine El Abidine Ben Ali and Libyan leader Muammar Gaddafi. EU concessions, for example on access to its market, were meant to reward them for steps towards good governance, if not democracy itself. In practice, however, they were often rewarded for steps to prevent people from crossing the Mediterranean.

Turkey, located to the south-east of the EU rather than across the Mediterranean, was a slightly different case. It had first signed an association agreement with the EEC in 1963 and finally applied to join the EC in 1987, the same year as Morocco—but unlike Morocco, was allowed to apply. However, the process was slow— ostensibly because of issues to do with Turkey's political institutions, human rights record, and treatment of minorities, especially the Kurds—and it was only in 1999 that it was finally given candidate status. Some member states, especially the UK, wanted Turkey in the EU for economic and strategic reasons. But others, such as France and Germany, had more fundamental reasons for opposing its membership of the EU that were based on an ethnic/cultural idea of what Europe was. This, in particular, illustrated how the EU continued to be informed by the medieval idea of a Europe that was synonymous with Christianity.[30]

Although the EU saw Turkey, unlike Morocco, as at least *potentially* European, the combination of its size and the cultural and religious identity of its population made it impossible for many Europeans to imagine it joining the EU. In 2002 Giscard D'Estaing, who was by then chairing the Convention on the Future of the European Union that was developing a new constitution for the EU and would be awarded the Charlemagne Prize the following year, said that Turkish accession would mean "the end of the European Union" and that those advocating for it were "the adversaries of the European Union".[31] Turkey had "a different culture, a different approach, a different way of life" and, in short, was "not a European country". He added that Turkish accession would also increase pressure to admit Morocco to the EU.

The opposition to the accession of a country with such a large Muslim population deepened as Islamophobia increased after 9/11 and subsequent terrorist attacks in Europe. In this context, the issue of Turkish accession was often framed in even more explicitly civilisational terms. In 2004, after the European Commission had published a report recommending opening accession talks with Turkey, European Commissioner Frits Bolkestein, a Dutch liberal who would play a leading role both in economic liberalisation in the EU and in the related "culturalization" of Dutch politics, echoed Giscard D'Estaing's warning that Turkish accession would be mean the end of the EU and put it in even more dramatic terms. He warned of an imminent "Islamisation" of Europe and even added that, if this happened, "the liberation of Vienna in 1683 would have been in vain".[32]

Olli Rehn, a supporter of Turkish membership, acknowledged that the real conditions for accession went "beyond the treaties".[33] Accession countries, he wrote, must also "win the acceptance of the European public". What he did not acknowledge, however, was that opposition to the accession of countries like Turkey from the public in many European countries was based as much on an ethnic/cultural idea of Europe as a civic one. Put simply, the EU implicitly differentiated between white and non-white countries—which undermined the idea of Europe as an inclusive project based on universal values. It showed that not only was the EU a regional rather than a cosmopolitan project, but that it defined its borders in ethnic/cultural terms.

Theorists of "cosmopolitan Europe", like Ulrich Beck, pointed to the way in which Europe was enlarging in the 2000s to show that European integration was an "open political project" and that "radical openness" was a defining feature of it. But this overlooked the reality that the EU, influenced by ethnic/cultural ideas of Europe, differentiated between east and south. Although "pro-Europeans" thought of the EU as "de-bordering" (that is, removing borders), it was also involved in "re-bordering" (that is, creating new borders).[34] It was true that internal borders had been removed (at least within the Schengen area). However, rather than removing the EU's external borders, enlargement had simply moved them further east, while the southern border remained where it was. This actually strengthened the identification of Europe, embodied by the EU, with whiteness.

*A return to whiteness?*

In central and eastern Europe, joining the EU was widely imagined as a "return to Europe". Yet this was an ambiguous phrase; "Europe" could mean many different things. The question, therefore, is what kind of imagined Europe central and eastern Europeans who joined the EU in 2004 thought they were becoming part of—and in what sense it was a "return" to something they had previously been part of. Partly because of the way in which "pro-Europeans" idealise the EU, they like to think that it was a purely civic version of European identity, one based on universalist values and in particular democracy. In reality, however, the Europe to which central and eastern Europeans imagined they were returning was one defined in ethnic/cultural terms as well as civic terms.

The ambiguity of the idea of a "return to Europe" went back to the nature of the revolutions of 1989 themselves. They are generally thought of as democratic revolutions—which of course they were. This is why many are now so baffled by the rollback of democracy in Hungary and Poland. However, as Branko Milanovic has argued, they were also nationalist revolutions whose aim was to create not just democratic but also ethnically homogenous nation states.[35] After World War II, central and eastern European countries had expelled people from ethnic minorities, they had not experienced mass immigration from outside Europe in the way that western European countries had, and they did not see ethnic heterogeneity as one of the "European values" to which they were committing themselves.

Nor did central and eastern European countries have the colonial histories of western European countries.

Rather, they had themselves been part of the Austro-Hungarian and Russian empires. In fact, the creation of small nations in central and eastern Europe after the end of World War I and the collapse of the Austro-Hungarian and Russian empires can be seen as the first decolonisation of the twentieth century.[36] However, it was not as if these new European nations showed much solidarity with anti-imperialist movements in countries in Africa and Asia that were themselves seeking independence. In fact, intellectuals in Czechoslovakia and Poland demanded that they be given extra-European colonies of their own—for them, that was part of what it meant to be a European nation.[37]

The Baltic states were annexed by the Soviet Union in 1940 and other central and eastern European countries came under Soviet control after the war—in other words, after decolonisation, they were recolonised. Even if Holocaust recognition was an unstated prerequisite for central and eastern European countries to join the EU, as Tony Judt suggested, they also expanded the EU's memory culture to include Stalinism as well as fascism.[38] Thus Beck and Grande wrote in 2007 that "the values and norms of the new Europe" were "an answer to the history of the regimes of terror of the twentieth century on both the left and right" and that "the experience of war and dictatorships, of the concentration camps and gulags of the twentieth century" were essential to the idea of "cosmopolitan Europe".[39]

Yet central and eastern European ideas of Europe were as much civilisational as political. For example, in an essay published in English in 1984 that would influence post-Cold War debates about the re-emergence of central Europe, Milan Kundera wrote that Europe was not a geographic space but a "spiritual notion synonymous with the word 'West'" that was opposed to Russia.[40] For Kundera the "tragedy" of central Europe was that it had been "kidnapped" by the Soviet Union and cut off from the western Europe to which it belonged. But this was not because he rejected civilisational thinking as such. Rather, it was because central Europe belonged to European civilisation—or was even the embodiment of it.[41] Furthermore, Western Europe had abandoned its cultural identity—which is why it did not feel the loss of central Europe. By returning to Europe, central Europeans would save it from itself.

In particular, what central and eastern European countries brought to the EU after they joined it was a renewed sense that Christianity was part of European identity. For example, during the final negotiations of the European constitution in 2004, the Czech Republic, Lithuania, Poland and Slovakia, which had officially joined the EU a month earlier, were among eight countries that sought to introduce a reference to "the Christian tradition" in the document's preamble.[42] (In the end the text referred to the "cultural, religious and humanist inheritance of Europe.") This emphasis on

Christianity recalled the Christian Democratic ideas of the 1950s and 1960s, in which Europe had been defined in opposition to the Soviet Union in both ideological and civilisational terms.

Thus, although enlargement increased the diversity of the EU during the post-Cold War period, it paradoxically also reinforced the sense of Europe as an exclusive space—one defined by culture and religion rather than by an exclusively civic identity.[43] Instead of overcoming the fault line between a "civilised" western Europe and a "barbaric" eastern Europe that went back to the Enlightenment, central and eastern European countries simply attempted to move the fault line further east than it had been during the Cold War so that they too were now part of the West. They sought to use the idea of central Europe to redeem themselves while using the trope of a backward eastern Europe to "perpetuate the exclusion of the rest", as Wolff puts it.[44]

József Böröcz has proposed the concept of "Eurowhiteness" to capture what he calls an "internal structuring of the category of 'Whiteness'".[45] In particular, he introduces a distinction "within the universe of 'Whiteness'" between "Eurowhiteness" and "dirty whiteness"—a category that denotes "less immaculate, either diasporic or 'eastern' variations of 'Whiteness'."[46] "Dirty whiteness" is aspirational; in response to what he calls "'eurowhite' condescension", it "embodies a demand for acceptance as properly 'White'." Böröcz suggests that the term applies particularly to central and eastern European countries. Joining the EU can be thought of as the expression of a desire to make a transition from "dirty whiteness" to "Eurowhiteness".

We can also use the term to refer to an ethnic/cultural idea of Europe, centred on the EU, which is related to the concept of whiteness but cannot be simply reduced to it. The Europe to which central and eastern European countries thought they were returning—with some justification given the difference between the EU's approaches to its eastern and its southern borders—was one that was still partly defined in civilisational terms. As Michael Wilkinson has put it: "The attitude of many of the new member states towards Europe was based on a distinct cultural myth, focused on shared Christian roots and historical alignment rather than political values".[47] In that sense, their "return to Europe" was also a return to Eurowhiteness.

## *The EU as a civilising power*

In the post-Cold War period, the EU also began to imagine itself as a power in international politics, but of a different kind than traditional "great powers". During the Cold War, the EEC and its successor, the EC, had had little in the way of an "external" policy—that is, a collective approach to the world beyond its own borders—except enlargement itself. But even as the EU was preoccupied with enlargement after the end of the Cold War, it also took a number of steps to create a more coherent foreign policy—and as it did so, it also began to conceptualise the kind of distinctive role it thought it might play in the world beyond Europe. The role that the EU imagined for itself was indicative both of its confidence during this period but also how it continued to be informed by the idea of a civilising mission.

Since the 1970s, EEC countries had cooperated on foreign policy only informally, through what was called European Political Cooperation. Since the EEC had formed a customs union in 1968, the European Commission set trade policy—particularly external tariffs. Beyond trade policy, however, member states tended to pursue separate foreign policies, and security policy cooperation worked largely through NATO. In 1992, however, the Maastricht Treaty committed the new EU to "assert its identity on the international scene" and created a Common Foreign and Security Policy. The Amsterdam Treaty in 1997 created a High Representative for Common Foreign and Security Policy—a kind of foreign minister for the EU, though one with few resources.

In part, this attempt to develop a more coherent foreign policy reflected the EU's confidence and ambition in the decade after the end of the Cold War. But it was also a response to the ethnic and regional conflicts that flared up in the 1990s, especially in the Balkans, which created a sense that a more coherent EU foreign policy was needed. When Jacques Poos, the foreign minister of Luxemburg, declared in June 1991—as Yugoslavia began to fall apart—that it was the "hour of Europe", it captured both of these factors. Finally, some "pro-Europeans", especially in France, also continued to resent American power and wanted to create a European bloc that was more independent of, and could act as a counterweight to, the United States.

Some "pro-Europeans" had already begun to try to conceptualise a distinctive role that Europe could play in international politics. In the early 1970s, François Duchêne, an advisor to Jean Monnet, had argued that, as "a civilian group of countries long on economic power and relatively short on armed force", the EC had an interest in trying to domesticate relations between states through "structures of contractual politics which have in the past been associated almost exclusively with 'home' and not foreign, that is, alien, affairs".[48] Later, this idea of "civilian power" was often thought simply to refer to an alternative to military power, but it was actually as much about the ends as the means. Primarily, a "civilian power" was one that sought to "civilise" international relations by strengthening international cooperation and international law.

This idea of civilising international politics went back to Kant's idea of "eternal peace". In particular, it meant "domesticating" international politics—turning it into something like domestic politics by establishing rules to govern the relations between states, in other words international law. The idea of "civilian power" also drew on the work of the German sociologist Norbert Elias on the "civilising process" that Europe had undergone from the medieval to the modern period, and in particular the way that the state's monopoly on the legitimate use of force had created pacified social spaces.[49] Theorists of "civilian power" sought to apply this civilising process to international politics, which—it was imagined—could also be "civilised" in the way European societies had been. A civilian power was therefore also a "civilising power".

After the end of the Cold War, there was renewed discussion about the EU as an actor in international politics. In particular, the idea of "normative power" emerged as a kind of successor to "civilian power".[50] It shared with it the idea that the EU was not simply pursuing the European interest—that is, a regional interest analogous to the national interest—but in doing so was transforming international relations in a way that was good for the whole world. Like the idea of "civilian power", it produced a tendency to idealise EU foreign policy and a lack of self-reflexivity.[51] It also created confusion between what "Europe" was perceived to stand for and the actions and structure of the EU itself. For example, although the EU itself might lack military capabilities, Europe did not—two EU member states even had nuclear weapons.

The idea of the EU as a normative power would remain a key element in debates on European foreign policy. But "pro-Europeans" now came to think that the EU needed a more traditional foreign policy and particularly needed to correct its deficit in military power. After Poos's declaration that it was the "hour of Europe", Dutch peacekeepers had failed to stop Serbian soldiers and paramilitaries carrying out a massacre at Srebrenica in 1995—which was particularly agonising for Europeans given the role that the Holocaust had come to play in the official narrative of the EU. EU member states depended on American military power to end the conflict in Bosnia and then again in the NATO intervention against Serbia in 1999, which was carried out without a mandate from the United Nations Security Council in the name of preventing a genocide against the Kosovar Albanians.

Following an Anglo-French agreement in 1998, the EU agreed to create a military force of 60,000 troops. The following year it launched a Common Security and Defence Policy (CSDP) and, just as the United States was about to invade Iraq in 2003, the EU deployed its first peacekeeping mission to the Former Yugoslav Republic of Macedonia. EU member states continued to use military force either on an ad hoc basis or through NATO, as they had in Kosovo in 1999 and would again in Afghanistan from 2001 onwards. But because these deployments did not take place through the EU itself, which only carried out softer operations, "pro-Europeans" could still imagine that "Europe" was an exceptionally peaceful power.

The invasion of Iraq in 2003 was an even bigger factor in galvanising momentum behind the idea of a European foreign policy and in crystallising a stylised contrast between a dovish Europe (or at least "Old Europe"—that is, the original Six) and a hawkish United States (as well as "New Europe"—that is, the member states that had joined subsequently).[52] Out of this moment came a revival of the idea of "Europe as revenge". In May 2003, Jürgen Habermas published an article, co-signed by the French philosopher Jacques Derrida, that argued that a new European consciousness was emerging from the opposition to the US-led invasion.[53] The Europe that Habermas described was one that stood for peace and international law and played, as Jan-Werner Müller put it, "the role of a 'civilizing' counterpart to the United States".[54]

This new momentum around the idea of a European foreign policy produced a further breakthrough with the Lisbon Treaty, which was signed in 2007. The treaty expanded the role of the High Representative and created a new diplomatic corps, the European External Action Service—a more powerful executive able to coordinate a more coherent European foreign policy. It was welcomed by "pro-Europeans" who wanted Europe to play a more forceful role in the world, thinking that it would not just be good for Europe but for the world because it would "civilise" international politics. Yet from a democratic perspective these new powers were deeply problematic: the Lisbon Treaty was a repackaged version of the European constitution that had been rejected by Dutch and French voters in 2005.

# 5

# THE CIVILISATIONAL TURN
# IN THE EUROPEAN PROJECT

The decade of crises that began with the euro crisis in 2010 transformed the EU. During the 2000s, as we saw in chapter 4, "pro-Europeans" had looked outward and imagined that they could civilise the world—by integrating central and eastern European countries, by developing countries in the EU's "neighbourhood", and by civilising international relations. But as the euro crisis exposed fundamental flaws within the EU itself and deep divisions between creditor and debtor countries while also creating instability in the global economy, it shook ideas of the EU as a model of regional integration. The EU then faced two external shocks in the form of political turmoil in north Africa and the Middle East and a Russia that was becoming more aggressive. In this context, the EU became more defensive as it came to see itself as being surrounded by threats.

Thus, in the first half of the 2010s, a more defensive Europe emerged. With the EU divided both between north and south and, after the refugee crisis in 2015, between east and south, there was a battle between different visions of Europe. Yet as the far right surged across the continent, the multiple threats to Europe were increasingly framed in civilisational terms. What emerged was a kind of defensive civilisationism that was reminiscent of, and drew on the memory of, earlier phases in European history in which Europeans had felt threatened—particularly the medieval period in which it had been threatened by Islam and the 1920s when the idea of a geopolitical Europe emerged.

In the second half of the 2010s, politics in Europe was widely seen in terms of a binary opposition between a "pro-European" centrism and a Eurosceptic "populism". But this binary way of thinking obscured the connections between the two. In response to the apparently inexorable rise of Eurosceptic "populism", "pro-European" centrists began to adopt far-right tropes and integrate them into the EU itself, producing a "pro-European" civilisationalism. By the beginning of the 2020s, the civic element of European regionalism seemed to have become less influential and the ethnic/cultural element more influential in "pro-European" thinking. In other words, whiteness seemed to be becoming more central to the European project.

## A defensive Europe

The euro crisis shattered the confidence that the EU had had for the previous two decades about its success and its role in the world. A bloc that had thought of itself as standing for prosperity and generous welfare states was now imposing apparently endless austerity. With the crisis came the return of conflicts within Europe, particularly between France and Germany, which were thought to have been part of European history—not least because European integration was itself supposed to have overcome them. In 2013, Jean-Claude Juncker, the former Luxembourg prime minister who would later become European Commission president, said that the situation in Europe was remarkably similar to that of a century before. "The demons haven't been banished," he said ominously.[1]

As a result of the euro crisis, the idea that the EU was a model for the rest of the world lost credibility. For decades, the EU had seen itself as a solution to the problems of a globalised world. But now, suddenly, it was itself a problem.[2] "Pro-Europeans" had long thought that, even if the EU did not have as much "hard power" as the United States, it had immense "soft power"—that is, it was "attractive" to others around the world—which had increased since the US-led invasion of Iraq.[3] The euro crisis, however, had made the EU "significantly less attractive as a model of governance for the rest of the world than it was", as a report by the European Council on Foreign Relations put it in 2012.[4] In other words, countries around the world and especially in the EU's "neighbourhood" were now less likely to adopt European "norms".

At the beginning of 2011, when pro-democracy protests began to sweep across north Africa and the Middle East, Europeans were initially hesitant even to support them—for example, when the uprising began in Tunisia, the French defence minister Michèle Alliot-Marie offered President Zine al Abidine Ben Ali the use of French security forces to suppress it.[5] After it became clear that authoritarian governments would fall, they pivoted and tried to support democratic transition—"Without Europe, there would still have been an Arab Spring, but without us there will be no Arab summer!" the President of the European Council, Herman van Rompuy, said—but without the prospect of accession that had been offered to central and eastern European countries. The new High Representative, Catherine Ashton, co-ordinated a strategy towards north Africa that aimed to develop what she called "deep democracy" in the region—that is, "respect for the rule of law, freedom of speech, an independent judiciary and impartial administration".[6]

As it had in central and eastern Europe, the EU sought to use conditionality—or, as Ashton put it, "more for more". It would offer "money, markets and mobility" in exchange for steps towards the development of the rule of law, freedom of speech, an independent judiciary and an impartial bureaucracy. As the EU struggled with the euro crisis, however, money was limited—in practice, much of it was in the form of loans rather than direct aid or debt cancellation. Because of southern European fears of competition from north African agricultural products, markets also remained largely closed off.[7] Finally, there was little desire to increase "mobility"—that is, immigration from north Africa. In fact, preventing migration flows would soon become the EU's main priority in north Africa, especially after the conflict in Syria worsened.

Unlike the revolutions in north Africa and the Middle East, which happened suddenly and wrong-footed Europeans, the threat from Russia emerged much more gradually—though this itself created another different problem for the EU. Russia had long been one of the most divisive foreign-policy issues in Europe, which had prevented the EU from developing a common approach to it. In particular, the EU was divided between Poland and the Baltic states, which saw Russia as a threat and wanted to a pursue a strategy of "soft containment", and other member states, especially Germany and Italy, which saw Russia as a potential partner that the EU could modernise and integrate—even after Russian President Vladimir Putin's rhetoric turned more aggressive from around 2007 onwards.[8]

After Russia annexed Crimea and invaded eastern Ukraine in 2014, and especially after Russian-backed rebels shot down an airliner over Ukraine that July, EU member states were able to agree on a set of economic sanctions against Russia, which, however, excluded the oil and gas imports from Russia on which several EU member states including Germany depended. But to deter Russia from further military action, either in Ukraine itself or against one of its member states, the EU continued to depend on the United States, which increased its military presence in Poland and the Baltic states even as it sought to "pivot" to the Asia-Pacific region and focus on the challenge of a rising China. Meanwhile, Chancellor Angela Merkel's government pushed ahead with Nord Stream 2, a new gas pipeline between Germany and Russia.

By the mid-2010s, these developments to the east and south had fused into a general sense that Europe was surrounded by threats. There was an "arc of instability" curving around the EU from east to south. Beyond the EU's "neighbourhood", there was also a wider sense that, far from international politics being "civilised" by the EU as "pro-Europeans" had hoped, the reverse was happening—that is, it was actually becoming more anarchic. Think tanks discussed the return of "geopolitics" or "great power politics" for which the EU, which many "pro-Europeans" still imagined as a "normative" power, was unprepared. Within the EU, therefore, there was both a new sense of insecurity and a sense that it needed to adapt to a new world.

In this context, a subtle but significant shift took place as the EU came to see itself less as a model and more as a *competitor*. In other words, rather than exporting its model to the rest of the world as it had hoped to in the 2000s, its priority was now to defend itself. However, there were different versions of this idea of competition. Some saw it in purely economic terms, others in more "geopolitical" terms, and others still in more civilisational terms. As always in the EU, what emerged was a compromise between these different visions. This centred, as it always had, on a negotiation between France and Germany. But unlike during the Cold War, France and Germany now also had to negotiate with "new Europe"—and this would be decisive for the future of the European project.

## *A "competitive" Europe*

The figure who embodied the idea of Europe as a competitor was Chancellor Angela Merkel, who talked endlessly of making Europe "competitive"—that is, able to compete economically, and perhaps by extension also geopolitically, with other regions in the world. She believed Europe needed to go even further than it already had in hollowing out the socio-economic model for which it once stood. In particular, she believed, it needed to cut back on the generous welfare states for which it was known. She liked to say that Europe had seven percent of the world's population, twenty-five per cent of its GDP and fifty per cent of its social spending in order to suggest that "it cannot continue to be so generous."[9]

This logic was behind the imposition of austerity on "crisis countries" in the eurozone. For example, Greek finance minister Yannis Varoufakis says that, in their first meeting, his German counterpart Wolfgang Schäuble wanted to talk about "the cuts that Europe had to make to its welfare state for it to compete with India and China".[10] But the welfare state and even the social market economy was being hollowed out not just in the eurozone "periphery" but also in its "core". As Oliver Nachtwey has shown, even as Germany underwent what some saw as a second "economic miracle" in the 2000s, labour had been weakened, the low-wage sector had grown to one of the largest in Europe, and "precariousness" had increased.[11]

Driven above all by Merkel, a kind of transformation of the EU also took place. It became more coercive—that is, coercion came to play a greater role than it previously had as a more extensive system of rules and their enforcement was created.[12] Conditionality—originally used in the context of the accession process and now used internally to discipline the eurozone "periphery"—was applied more strictly.[13] EU documents used the language of "surveillance" and "discipline".[14] There was still a kind of "solidarity" within the EU, but it was the kind of solidarity that the International Monetary Fund

(IMF) showed to countries that it assisted—that is, loans in exchange for structural reforms (or "structural adjustment" in IMF terms).[15]

Against this background, European politics also changed. In debtor countries, the political centre was hollowed out and new anti-austerity parties emerged, like Syriza in Greece which came to power in January 2015. Meanwhile, in creditor countries, far-right parties like the Alternative für Deutschland (AfD) emerged which believed that the EU, led by Germany, had already gone too far towards a "transfer union"—that is, one in which fiscally responsible countries subsidised fiscally irresponsible ones. Thus Euroscepticism increased in both creditor and debtor countries as the EU remained "entrapped".[16] "Pro-Europeans" generally responded by closing ranks even more tightly against what they saw as a wave of left-wing and right-wing "populism".

Although southern Europe opposed the German-led approach to the euro crisis and the way it was transforming the EU, central and eastern European countries were generally supportive. Since the end of the Cold War and especially since they joined the EU in 2004, their economies had been integrated into the German manufacturing supply chain, particularly in the automobile industry, turning them into "an assembly plant for German companies", as Konrad Popławski has put it.[17] This produced a kind of geo-economic equivalent of a German sphere of influence in which central and eastern European countries saw their national interests as being mostly aligned with Germany's.[18] When the Greek debt crisis flared up again in July 2015, central and eastern European countries that were in the eurozone like Slovakia were vocal in supporting Germany in its aggressive approach.[19]

However, this relationship between Germany and central and eastern European countries changed with the refugee crisis a few months later. It suddenly created a new fault line between western and eastern member states perpendicular to the existing fault line between northern and southern member states, based not on economic issues but cultural ones. As hundreds of thousands of asylum seekers, many of them from Syria, made their way through Europe towards Germany, it proposed a plan to "relocate" 120,000 of them to other member states based on mandatory quotas. However, despite their economic dependence on Germany, the Visegrád 4 (the Czech Republic, Hungary, Poland and Slovakia) joined forces to vehemently oppose the plan—especially after the far-right Law and Justice party (PiS) came to power in Poland in October 2015.[20]

In the refugee crisis, it was Germany that needed other EU member states to show solidarity with it by accepting what it saw as their "fair share" of asylum seekers. But central and eastern European countries responded in a way that echoed how Germany had responded to demands for solidarity from debtor countries in the euro crisis. Just as Merkel had insisted that the euro crisis was a problem of indebted countries that needed to implement austerity and structural reform, so Hungarian prime minister Viktor Orbán insisted that the refugee crisis was a "German problem", not a European one.[21] He even accused Germany of "moral imperialism" in the same way that debtor countries had accused it of "fiscal imperialism" in the context of the euro crisis.[22]

The dramatic battle between Merkel and Orbán over refugees made them seem like opposites—Merkel the figurehead of "liberalism" and Orbán the figurehead of "illiberalism". But this was misleading. Although Merkel was said to have "opened Germany's borders" in the summer of 2015, the reality was that Germany was unable to stop the flow of asylum seekers—and she subsequently negotiated a deal with Turkey that in effect outsourced the management of the EU's borders to an "illiberal" or even authoritarian state. Conversely, Orbán was quite liberal in economic terms. He too spoke the language of "competitiveness"—in fact he said that it was precisely in order to be "competitive" that Hungary needed to be "illiberal".[23]

Moreover, the German Christian Democrats and Fidesz, Orbán's party, remained in the same grouping within the European Parliament, the European People's Party (EPP); in other words, they were allies. While they disagreed on the "relocation" of asylum seekers within the EU, they had shared economic interests in the "competitive" Europe that had emerged from the euro crisis. The tendency to think of European politics in terms of a struggle between a liberalism that was identified with the EU and an illiberalism that was identified with Euroscepticism obscured the way that, particularly in central Europe, the centre right and the far right were converging. As a result, far-right ideas would increasingly shape the agenda of the EU itself.

## *Macron and* L'Europe qui protège

In May 2017, just under a year after the British people had voted to leave the EU, Emmanuel Macron was elected as president of France with a different vision of Europe. Macron had framed the presidential election as a choice between "pro-Europeanism" and Euroscepticism—and, more broadly, between centrism and "populism". The Brexit vote had confirmed to Macron that the EU was at the centre of a new ideological battle between "open" and "closed" visions. He identified the EU with "open" societies and an "open" world and both left-wing and right-wing Eurosceptics with the idea of "closed" societies and a "closed" world. As an electoral strategy against Front National leader Marine Le Pen, against whom he ran in the second round of the election, it was successful.

Despite this rhetoric about "openness", Macron's vision for Europe was centred on the idea of "protection"—a direct response to the increasing sense of being threatened that pervaded Europe. In a speech at the Sorbonne in September 2017, he proposed a *Europe qui protège*, or "Europe that protects", in which the eurozone would be reformed to protect citizens from the market. Shortly after becoming president, he warned central and eastern European countries not to treat Europe (by which he obviously meant the EU) "as a supermarket".[24] He negotiated a reform of the Posted Workers Directive, an EU rule that had been perceived in France as "social dumping"—that is, the lowering of standards through competition. Central and eastern European countries in turn understood *L'Europe qui protège* as essentially protectionist.

Initially, therefore, *L'Europe qui protège* was a centre-left idea that focused on economic protection. Before forming his own new party, En Marche, in 2016, Macron had been economics minister in the socialist government of François Hollande. During the election campaign, he had claimed to be a radical centrist who was "ni gauche, ni droite" ("neither left nor right"). After becoming president, however, he seemed to govern from the right—in particular, he scrapped a wealth tax and liberalised the labour market—and was thus seen as "president of the rich".[25] The thinking in the Elysée was that if France reformed its economy it would gain credibility in Berlin, which would in turn mean that Macron could persuade Germany to agree to a more redistributive EU.

The idea of *L'Europe qui protège* was in effect a last attempt to save the idea of a "social Europe" that had been central to the French centre left's approach to the European project. Since the presidency of François Mitterrand in the 1980s, the French centre left had believed that social democratic economic policies were now only possible at the European level. But France had always struggled to persuade Germany to pursue a centre-left economic policy, especially after the creation of the European single currency, which had constitutional-ised German preferences by limiting the ability of governments to borrow and spend. Having failed to cajole Germany into making concessions during the Hollande government, Macron now sought to try again with what he saw as a new strategy.

At the same time, however, *L'Europe qui protège* was also about protecting Europe from the rest of the world. The election of Donald Trump as US president in November in 2016 had created radical uncertainty about the US security guarantee to Europe and led many "pro-Europeans", somewhat strangely, to see the power on which they depended for their security as yet another threat. (Similarly, although the EU also depended on the UK as a secondary security provider, some also saw it as a threat or even as part of the "arc of instability" that surrounded the EU.)[26] This, together with the perception of threats from a revisionist Russia and a rising China, led to a revival of the idea of a "geopolitical" Europe that went back to the 1920s.

In particular, there was much discussion about European "strategic autonomy"—the idea that the EU should be independent of the United States in security terms. "Pro-Europeans" also began talking about "European sovereignty".[27] In the past, they had rejected the concept of sovereignty as either anachronistic or dangerous and criticised other powers, including the United States, for being too "sovereigntist". But as the EU became more defensive, they began to embrace it. Thus when the Trump administration imposed new sanctions against Iran, which would also affect European companies, it was seen as a violation of "European sovereignty".[28] Through a series of interviews and speeches, Macron became the leading spokesperson for this idea of a more "autonomous" or "sovereign" Europe.

However, Germany responded neither to Macron's proposals for eurozone reform nor to his ideas for a more independent EU. Although many in Berlin had been spooked by how well Le Pen had done in the 2017 election and realised that Germany needed Macron to succeed, Germany was simply not willing to make concessions in either policy area. Therefore Merkel simply ignored Macron's proposals for reform of the eurozone. Nor did she do much to help the EU become more "autonomous" or "sovereign"; while in a speech in 2018 she said that Europe could no longer depend on the United Kingdom or the United States and needed to "take its destiny in its own hands", she did little to increase defence spending or reduce Germany's economic and energy dependence on China and Russia.

When Macron had run for election in 2017, he had generally been perceived as being on the left on cultural issues, even if he was already seen as being somewhat right-wing on economic issues. Despite the series of horrific terrorist attacks that had taken place in France, including the Bataclan massacre in November 2015 which led to the imposition of a state of emergency, he did not seek to exploit them. After becoming president, he did introduce measures to make it harder to apply for asylum in France and did little to assist Italy and Greece, where, after the so-called Balkan route had been shut down in 2016, asylum seekers were now arriving in large numbers after crossing the Mediterranean in small boats. But he rejected Orbán's vision of a Christian Europe and criticised member states that refused to accept the "relocation" of asylum seekers, whom Orbán called "Muslim invaders".[29]

However, after getting nowhere with Germany, Macron's approach to cultural questions changed. In the autumn of 2019, he gave an interview to the far-right magazine *Valeurs Actuelles* and was pictured on the cover of the magazine with the headline: "The failure of our model is combined with the crisis that Islam is going through." Following the murder of the teacher Samuel Paty by an eighteen-year-old of Chechen origin the following year, and under increasing pressure from Le Pen,

Macron took steps to stop what he called "Islamist separatism". In particular, he introduced measures to increase state control over mosques and imams in France to "defend the republic and its values". In other words, *L'Europe qui protège* had been reinvented in terms of cultural rather than economic protection.

## *The European Way of Life*

The evolution of Macron's idea of *L'Europe qui protège* was a condensed version of what was happening across Europe, as political contestation shifted from economic to cultural issues. The far right was becoming stronger, particularly since the refugee crisis, and the centre right was mimicking its rhetoric and policies, particularly on questions of identity, Islam and immigration, and creating a "pro-European" version of them—what might be called "ethnoregionalism", as I suggested in chapter 1. What this convergence between the centre right and the far right produced was an EU that was based on a mixture of Merkel's vision of a "competitive" Europe and Orbán's vision of a Christian Europe—in other words a Europe that was neoliberal in economic terms and protectionist in cultural terms.

In an EU that was now divided between east and west as well as north and south, the far right seemed to on the rise everywhere. In Germany, the AfD had reinvented itself as an anti-immigrant party after the refugee crisis and not only entered the Bundestag for the first time in 2017 but, after the formation of the third grand coalition in four electoral periods, became the biggest opposition party. In southern European countries, where it had mainly been new left-wing parties that had emerged in the first half of the 2010s, the far right now also began to surge—in particular in Italy, where the Lega joined a government led by the "techno-populist" Five Star Movement in 2018.[30] In response to this rise, centre-right politicians adopted elements of the far right's agenda, as Mark Rutte did in the Netherlands, or formed coalitions with far-right parties, as Sebastian Kurz did in Austria.[31]

Against the background of this blurring of the distinction between the centre right and the far right in Europe, "pro-Europeans" began to think in increasingly civilisational terms. In his 1996 book *The Clash of Civilisations*, Samuel Huntington had predicted conflict between the West and China and Islam. Influenced by Huntington, some had already thought in terms of a clash of civilisations in the period after 9/11, as Frits Bolkestein's comments on Turkish membership illustrated.[32] As the EU saw the threats to it in cultural terms in the second half of the 2010s, this kind of civilisational thinking became even more prevalent. But whereas Atlanticists thought in terms of Western civilisation, as Huntington did, many "pro-Europeans", drawing on a tradition going back to the 1920s, imagined Europe as a civilisation that was distinct from, and even threatened by, the United States.

In 2019, the German Christian Democrat Ursula von der Leyen became the new president of the European Commission. The defence minister in Merkel's cabinet, she had not been one of the so-called *Spitzenkandidaten*, or lead candidates, who stood for election—a new innovation introduced five years earlier to give the European Commission more democratic legitimacy. But she was seen as a passionate "pro-European", was proposed by Macron as a compromise candidate, and was elected with the help of votes from PiS and Fidesz, which was still part of the EPP even though the EU was taking action against Hungary for undermining the rule of law.[33] Von der Leyen promised a "geopolitical" Commission.[34] Although it was far from clear what she meant by that—was it a return to the 1920s idea of a geopolitical Europe?—the idea would be embraced by "pro-Europeans" as a shorthand for a more powerful Europe.[35]

Von der Leyen's new Commission included as one of its vice-presidents Margaritis Schinas, a Greek official who would be responsible among other things for migration policy and whose title was Commissioner for Promoting Our European Way of Life. When the new position had initially been proposed, its title had included the word "protecting", which had become popular since Macron had used it, but after objections by some members of the European Parliament, the

Commission agreed to change it to the less-defensive "promoting".[36] What was really troubling about the new commissioner's title, however, was not the exact choice of verb but rather the concept of the European Way of Life itself and in particular the connection of the phrase with migration.

The European Way of Life was an ambiguous phrase that could refer to a European identity that was either civic or ethnic/cultural or a mixture of both. During an earlier phase in the European project, some "pro-Europeans" had used the phrase to capture the EU's socio-economic model, and in particular the principle of solidarity it expressed—in other words a more civic idea of Europe. In 2001, for example, the Socialist French prime minister Lionel Jospin had spoken of a specific European way of life based on this model.[37] But the connection of the phrase with migration made it clear that the EU now understood the European way of life in a much more cultural way. It made it explicit that migration was not just a difficult issue to be managed but a threat to the European Way of Life.

Above all, this defensive civilisationalism led to a transformation of the EU's approach to its southern "neighbourhood". During its earlier, more optimistic period, the EU had aspired to transform north African countries using trade, aid and technical support. Yet as its policy towards the region became focused on reducing the drivers of migration, especially after 2015, it went from what Roderick Parkes calls "high-handed engagement" to protectionism. "The EU's posture towards its neighbors can increasingly be explained by one thing: fear of migrants," Parkes wrote in 2020.[38] The EU expanded Frontex, the border agency which it proudly declared was its first uniformed service, and took more aggressive steps to stop migrants reaching Europe, including illegal "pushbacks"—which it also covered up.[39]

The threats from migration and authoritarian powers in the EU's "neighbourhood" would merge in the form of the idea of the "weaponisation" of migration. Amid recriminations between the EU and Turkey over the implementation of the deal agreed in 2016, Turkish president Recep Tayyip Erdoğan threatened to allow refugees to cross into Greece. In May 2021, after Spain provided medical assistance to a leader of the Western Sahara independence movement, the Moroccan government allowed around a thousand people to enter the Spanish enclave of Ceuta. Later in the year, after the EU imposed sanctions on Belarus, it escorted thousands of asylum seekers to approach the Polish border, where they were violently pushed back. Officials like Schinas began to refer to migration as a "hybrid threat"—language that signalled a further militarisation of the EU's borders.

The EU's defensive civilisationism would also inform wider European foreign policy debates. The sense of being surrounded by threats had informed the debate about "strategic autonomy" and "European sovereignty". But the idea of a "geopolitical" Europe was now also increasingly being seen in civilisational terms. In a speech setting out his vision of French foreign policy to a gathering of France's ambassadors around the world in Paris in 2019, Macron spoke about the need for the EU, led by France, to pursue what he called a "project of European civilisation".[40] He distinguished European civilisation from American civilisation, which he said did not share the same humanism, and Chinese civilisation, which did not share the same values.

Macron said France's objective must be to "refound" European civilisation and make the EU a *puissance d'équilibre*, or balancing power, between China and the United States—a twenty-first century version of the Cold War notion of Europe as a "third force" in international politics. If the EU did not take bold action, he warned darkly, "Europe will disappear". Thus, debates about European foreign policy resembled a kind of international political equivalent of debates about immigration based on the fear of the "great replacement". Just as white replacement theory was based on the fear of "ethnic disappearance", the foreign policy debate was animated by the analogous idea that, unless Europeans united and asserted themselves in the world, they would be replaced by other powers.

## *The war in Ukraine*

The Russian invasion of Ukraine in February 2022 was a strategic shock for the EU. Although the conflict in the Donbas region of eastern Ukraine had been going on for almost a decade since 2014, the EU was largely unprepared for Vladimir Putin's dramatic escalation. Poland and the Baltic states had long urged the EU to take a tougher approach to Russia and to provide Ukraine with more support, but this had been resisted by other member states like France and Germany. "The world is no longer the same as it was before", the new German chancellor Olaf Scholz said in a speech two days after the invasion.[41] It was a way of framing the Russian invasion that exonerated Germany; rather than admitting that it had made mistakes, especially by failing to reduce its dependence on Russian gas even after 2014, Scholz implied that the situation had now simply changed.

It was also a rather Eurocentric way of framing the crisis. After all, as well as the conflict in the Donbas, there had also been plenty of other conflicts around the world during the last decade that indicated that international politics was becoming more fraught—not least the conflict in Syria, in which half a million had died since it broke out in 2011, in part due to the military support provided by Russia to President Bashar al-Assad. Yet the conflict in Ukraine was seen as being different from these other conflicts elsewhere in the world.

Analysts, commentators and reporters expressed shock that such a brutal conflict could have happened in "civilised" Europe—implicitly opposed to the "uncivilised" world beyond where such conflict was somehow normal or could not be prevented.

The war in Ukraine further strengthened the sense that Europe was threatened, solidifying the consensus that the EU needed to become more "geopolitical" or "learn to speak the language of power", as the High Representative Josep Borrell put it, though what exactly this meant also remained unclear.[42] The war illustrated again how dependent the EU was on the United States, and to a lesser extent on the UK, for its security. But Scholz announced a massive increase in German defence spending and for the first time the EU also jointly financed the purchase and delivery of weapons, which was seen as a major breakthrough. The EU also began to take steps to reduce its dependence on Russian energy, including buying gas from other producers, which in turn produced sudden shortages in developing countries.

Having previously hesitated to support Ukraine in economic, political and military terms, the EU now suddenly and wholeheartedly embraced it. Ukraine was widely seen as defending, or fighting for, Europe or "European values". European Commission president Ursula von der Leyen declared that Ukrainians were "one of us" and "belong to us" and promised to help it join the EU as soon as possible.[43] Yet von der Leyen and other "pro-Europeans" did not spell out exactly what kind of Europe or European values Ukraine was thought to be defending or fighting. The idea of "European values" was rather nebulous and malleable—in particular, it now apparently included territorial integrity and even state sovereignty, concepts that the EU was traditionally seen as blurring or transcending.

Echoing the way that the revolutions in central and eastern Europe in 1989 were perceived, Ukraine's struggle against Russia was seen above all in democratic rather than nationalist terms. It was perceived this way despite the complicated, problematic history of Ukrainian nationalism in the twentieth century and even the uncomfortable fact that since 2014 much of the fighting in the Donbas had been done by the Azov Battalion, a neo-Nazi militia that had been integrated into the Ukrainian National Guard and whose soldiers were presumably not exactly fighting for a civic idea of Europe.[44] One senior Ukrainian official told the BBC that what made the situation so emotional for him was that it was "European people with blue eyes and blonde hair" who were being killed.[45]

This kind of racialised response to the war also seemed to influence the EU's approach to the refugees from Ukraine. Even as the EU continued to brutally push back migrants in the Mediterranean, it opened its borders to those fleeing from Ukraine and provided them with extraordinary support.[46] The contrast between the generosity shown towards refugees from Ukraine and the way that refugees from Africa and the Middle East were treated was particularly extreme in the case of Poland. Some hoped that this might be the beginning of a new, more humane EU approach to asylum seekers in general. In reality, the policy that the PiS government was now pursuing was not different from the one it had pursued during the refugee crisis in 2015—a policy based on a sense of ethnic/cultural solidarity.[47]

In the months after the Russian invasion, calls for a more "geopolitical" Europe were often framed in civilisational terms. For example, in a speech in May 2022, Borrell said: "If we want to protect European civilisation, we must unify."[48] In this context, "pro-Europeans" also tended to construct Russia as a civilisational as well as ideological Other—similar to the perception of the Soviet Union during the Cold War, as we saw in chapter 3. For example, Florence Gaub, the deputy director of the European Union Institute for Security Studies, the EU's own foreign policy think tank, declared on German television that Russians might "look European" but were not European "in a cultural sense" because they did not value human life in the same way as Europeans.[49]

There was also much speculation about a transformation of the political dynamics within the EU. In particular, analysts diagnosed a shift in the EU's centre of gravity away from France and Germany, which were widely believed to have lost moral authority and credibility because of their failure to take a tougher approach to deterring Russia, and central and eastern European countries like Poland, which were believed to have been prescient and felt vindicated.[50] Until the war began, the EU had been locked in a dispute with both Hungary and Poland over the rule of law. After the war began, the EU continued to take action against Orbán, who was seen as an ally of Putin. But it sought to accommodate Poland, which was now suddenly seen as a frontline member state standing for the same "European values"—in particular, democracy—that it had previously been seen as rejecting.

Many "pro-Europeans" viewed the war in Ukraine as a transformative moment for the EU. Many saw it in particular as an opportunity to "reinvent" or "refound" the EU. The war in Ukraine seemed to have given the EU "a newfound sense of purpose", as Borrell put it, and demonstrated that it was a *Schicksalsgemeinschaft*, or "community of fate".[51] Yet at this moment when "pro-Europeans" wanted to remake the EU, the far right was ascendant in Europe—and Poland, with a far-right government, was playing an increasingly influential role in the EU. The war in Ukraine clearly made the EU even more defensive than it had already become during the decade of crises that began with the euro crisis in 2010. It remains to be seen whether it will also turn out to have strengthened the civilisational turn in the European project.

# 6

# BREXIT AND IMPERIAL AMNESIA

Brexit has been widely understood as an expression of white anger. It is seen as a nativist revolt, a rejection of the diversity and openness for which the EU is thought to stand, and an expression of nostalgia for empire. Just as Donald Trump channelled racism among white Americans yearning for an earlier period in American history, so Brexit has been widely seen as expressing a yearning among British people for a time before mass immigration began in the 1950s—in other words, a white Britain. In the phrase "Global Britain", the Conservative government's slogan for the UK's role in the world after leaving the EU, many have also seen a neo-imperial project, as if the UK were hoping or planning somehow to reacquire colonies. Some critics of Brexit have even spoken of "Empire 2.0".

This view of Brexit is part of a wider tendency among centrists since 2016 to see the world in extremely simplistic binary terms. In particular, politics has been viewed in terms of a struggle between liberalism and illiberalism, nationalism and internationalism, or even "open" and "closed" visions of society and the world—which, ironically, mimics the binary worldview of the populists that centrists criticise. In fact, centrists often think in terms of the same binary oppositions—for example between nationalism and globalism. Central to this binary view of the world is the concept of populism, and Brexit has been seen through this prism. But unlike the other figures, movements and parties around the world that have been called populist, Brexit is a *decision*—which makes its meaning much more elusive.

In this final chapter, I argue that the meaning of Brexit is much more complex and open-ended than is suggested by the idea of a nativist revolt analogous to that which produced Trump. For some among Britain's ethnic minority population who voted to leave the EU, for example, it was not so much an expression of racism but its opposite—a rejection of a bloc that they saw as racist. The long, complex story of the UK's relationship with the Commonwealth and what became the EU—and in particular the change in its immigration policy after it joined—suggests that Brexit can also be understood as a rebalancing rather than a rejection of immigration. I conclude by arguing that Brexit can also be seen as an opportunity for the UK to deepen its engagement with its colonial past.

## *The elusiveness of Brexit*

It is almost impossible to capture the meaning of Brexit. All kinds of different arguments were made for leaving the EU from political actors of different kinds. There were left-wing arguments for leaving the EU as well as right-wing ones, though this is often forgotten or dismissed, as well as arguments that are difficult to classify in left/right terms, such as those around democracy and sovereignty. In the referendum in June 2016, 17.4 million people voted to leave the EU. The research on their reasons for voting to leave the EU reveals an extremely complex picture—though that has not prevented many commentators and analysts in the UK and beyond from making simplistic and misleading judgements about the meaning of Brexit.

To begin with, it is necessary to distinguish between the supply and demand sides of politics—that is, between political entrepreneurs on the one hand and voters on the other. The gap between what campaigners and politicians were offering and what voters wanted was particularly large in the case of the referendum. Voters were not making a choice between parties with manifestos setting out policy positions, but rather answering the simple question of whether to leave or remain in the EU. Nevertheless, the meaning of Brexit is often simply reduced either to the views of individual figures like Nigel Farage, or alternatively to certain subsets of the 17.4 million people who voted to leave the EU, such as the "white working class".

Even if the focus is restricted to political entrepreneurs, the picture is complicated. There were two campaigns: the official Vote Leave campaign, which was supported by Conservative politicians such as Boris Johnson and focused more on economic arguments for leaving the EU; and the unofficial campaign founded by Arron Banks, which focused more on immigration. UK Independence Party leader Nigel Farage also in effect ran his own campaign—including the notorious "Breaking Point" poster which depicted a queue of non-white people, perhaps asylum seekers. This poster was frequently cited as evidence of the perceived racism of Brexit, even though the issue on which the referendum would have an impact was freedom of movement (that is, immigration from within the EU) rather than asylum policy.

Although Johnson and Farage spoke about British history in problematic terms, it is too easy to see them as yearning for empire. As Robert Saunders has shown, the reality of the ways in which empire has been "remembered, articulated and forgotten in arguments for or against European integration" is far more complicated than the idea of Brexit as a neo-colonial project suggests.[1] Rather than celebrating empire, let alone imagining a new version of it, right-wing Leavers tended to minimise its significance in British history. They had a "heroic vision of British history that was *global* rather than *imperial*" and tended to talk not so much of a revived empire but of an Anglosphere based on a fetishisation of free trade.[2] The problem was not so much imperial nostalgia as imperial *amnesia*—in other words, a *forgetting* of empire rather than a longing for it.[3]

The memory of empire also informed the thinking of Remainers. Among those who have spoken positively about the British empire, for example, are David Cameron and Tony Blair.[4] In particular, many Remainers saw membership of the EU as a way for the UK to continue to "punch above its weight" after the loss of empire. Such arguments went back to the first referendum in 1975, when leading figures in the Yes campaign argued that only the EC would allow the UK to retain its power and influence in the world after the loss of its colonies. Margaret Thatcher, the Conservative party leader, argued explicitly that membership of the EC would allow the UK to continue its role in "civilising" the world.[5] Thus Europe became, as Saunders puts it, "a new vehicle for the UK's imperial ambitions".[6]

Discussion of the demand side of Brexit—that is, voters' motivations for voting to leave the EU—has generally centred on a debate between the relative importance of economic and cultural causes of populism. Economic factors include wage stagnation, the loss of manufacturing jobs, increased inequality and economic insecurity or "precariousness". Cultural factors include opposition to progressive value change since the 1960s, anger about immigration, and racism and Islamophobia. Although in the initial period after the referendum in 2016, the debate was often framed in terms of competition between cultural and economic causes, a consensus has now emerged that the two sets of factors played a role and interacted in complex ways.

Some political scientists have seen a particular parallel between the cultural causes of Brexit and the election of Trump as US president in 2016.[7] In such analyses, attitudes to immigration in the UK are seen as being analogous to the racial resentment which clearly contributed to the election of Trump.[8] However, there are reasons to think the two cases are somewhat different. At the centre of the debate about immigration in the context of Brexit was freedom of movement within the EU rather than legal or illegal immigration of people from outside the EU, which made it quite different from the immigration debate in the United States. This makes it harder to see concerns about immigration as a straightforward expression of racism against non-white people or of a fear of the UK becoming a majority-minority country.

The more compelling parallel may be in terms of economic causes of Brexit and Trump. The United States and the UK have followed remarkably similar economic trajectories going back to Margaret Thatcher and Ronald Reagan, which help to explain some of the anger expressed by those who voted for Brexit and Trump. In particular, neoliberal economic policy since the 1980s led in both cases to a massive increase in inequality even beyond that elsewhere in the West. In both countries, areas that had specialised in manufacturing were hit hard by competition from emerging economies—especially from the "China shock", which research has shown played a role in the political polarisation that led to Brexit and Trump.[9]

However, thinking of Brexit in terms of cultural and economic causes leaves little space for the concerns around democracy which were central to the debate about British membership of the EU. Voter concerns about "sovereignty" were often seen in terms of *national* sovereignty and thus understood as indicating authoritarian (as opposed to libertarian) values—especially because of the way in which the EU was identified with "cosmopolitanism". But these concerns were also about *popular* sovereignty, which many British people saw, rightly or wrongly, as going hand in hand with national sovereignty. Thus concerns about sovereignty could indicate not so much an "authoritarian reflex", as some who looked at Brexit through the prism of "populism" saw it, but a "democratic reflex" and in particular a sense that democracy had been hollowed out.

Finally, as well as analyses of campaigns or voter behaviour, there have also been important attempts to understand the deep causes of Brexit. For example, Helen Thompson has argued that Brexit was in a sense inevitable because of the way that the relationship between the UK and the EU evolved after the euro crisis began in 2010, which "put a time-bomb under the sustainability of Britain's membership of the EU".[10] In particular, she argues, "the political economy generated by Britain's position as a non-euro member of the EU while possessing the offshore financial centre of the eurozone" made Brexit "an eventual inevitability".[11] However, though it may have been inevitable that the UK would sooner or later leave the EU, its future outside of the EU remains open ended.

## The EU as a "white fortress"

One key and under-discussed element of the Brexit story that challenges, or at least complicates, the idea that it was an expression of racism is the complex attitudes of Britain's ethnic minority population to the EU.[12] In the referendum, a third of black and Asian Britons voted to leave the EU—that is, around a million people.[13] Many seem to have done so for the same set of reasons as white voters. But qualitative research since the referendum has shown that, for some non-white British citizens, their unique experiences of racism in continental Europe and perceptions of the racism of the EU itself contributed to their choices. Thus, for at least *some* British citizens, Brexit was not so much an expression of white anger as the opposite: the rejection of a bloc that was itself perceived as being racist.

As Neema Begum has shown, many of those from ethnic minorities in the UK who voted to leave did so because they saw other EU member states as "more racist or Islamophobic" and believed that "minority rights were better protected in Britain".[14] They believed that, as ethnic and religious minorities, they would be better off out of the EU "because they saw other European countries as being more racist".[15] In particular, some Muslim women were "more concerned by the hijab and burkini bans put in place in some member states than they were reassured by EU attempts to promote gender equality". Their perceptions of the EU were also shaped by the refugee crisis—not in the sense that they feared asylum seekers but that they were troubled by the EU's treatment of them.

Beyond the issue of asylum policy, the views of non-white Leavers complicate conventional narratives about the role that immigration played in the decision to leave the EU. In particular, non-white Leavers often saw freedom of movement within the EU as a form of indirect discrimination against non-white people. They were troubled by what they saw as a striking contrast between the ease with which EU citizens could move to and work in the UK, compared to the difficulty they had in bringing their own family members from Commonwealth countries to live in the UK—or even to visit. As a result, they saw the EU as a "white fortress" that facilitated white immigration while obstructing the entry of non-white people.[16]

Two-thirds of non-white British citizens voted to remain in the EU. Yet even they tended not to identify strongly as European. "They saw being European as a white identity and felt it didn't include them", Begum writes.[17] Appeals to the idea of a shared European identity did not resonate with ethnic minorities in the UK, who identified more strongly as British than as European.[18] Whereas white Remainers often saw the EU as the embodiment of openness and progressiveness, these perceptions were not shared by those from ethnic minorities in the UK. Rather, they saw a kind of "white protectionism"—by preventing non-white people coming to Europe but also through economic policies like the Common Agricultural Policy, which they saw as subsidising European farmers while having devastating effects on farming in Africa.[19]

Other qualitative research has also documented the experiences of non-white British people who have lived elsewhere in the EU.[20] Often, they described moving to continental Europe as a "culture shock".[21] Although many also experienced racism in the UK, they felt that in continental Europe they experienced racism of a more virulent kind and perceived a lower awareness of racism in general. One interviewee compared it to "different levels of atmospheric pressure" and said that when he travelled to some European countries he would "get the bends"—that is, the sickness caused by a sudden change in pressure.[22] In particular, interviewees described racism in continental European countries as being of a kind that had long ceased to exist in the UK. In short, they saw continental Europe as lagging behind the UK in addressing racism.

Central and eastern European countries are perceived as being particularly hostile to non-white people. In fact, in a BBC documentary in 2012, the English footballer Sol Campbell discouraged non-white England fans from attending the upcoming European championship in Poland and Ukraine because of the danger of racial attacks.[23] Two black members of the England squad said their families would not attend because of such fears. Even the Foreign Office advised travelling fans of African-Caribbean or Asian descent to take "extra care". The point here is not so much whether such advice was justified, but rather that the perception among many non-white Britons is that continental Europe—and in particular central and eastern Europe—is more racist than the UK.

Non-white British citizens have also described their experiences of racism within the EU institutions themselves.[24] One consequence of the UK's withdrawal from the EU was to dramatically reduce the number of non-white people working within the EU institutions.[25] In particular, it seems to have dramatically reduced the number of non-white MEPs in the European Parliament, though there are no exact figures because member states such as France and Germany do not collect ethnic data.[26]

That lack of data in turn strengthens the perception among non-white British people that continental Europe lags far behind the UK in terms of addressing the problem of racism—and that the EU itself is a part of the problem rather than the solution.

Few of the other advances that the UK is perceived to have made in terms of addressing the problem of racism had much to do with membership of the EU either. The UK introduced its first legislation outlawing racial discrimination in 1965—in other words, before it joined the EC and at a time when few other European countries had such legislation and the EU itself had not even begun to address the question of racism.[27] One of the arguments made in favour of remaining in the EU, especially by the left, was that it had guaranteed rights for British citizens. But even if this was true in other areas, there was little sense among the UK's non-white communities that the EU had helped protect them from racism or that they would be less protected if the UK left the EU.

## The UK between empire and Europe

The historical context for these perceptions of the EU and the question of British membership of it is the gradual shift away from the Commonwealth to Europe as a focus for British ambition and identity since World War II—in other words, the way in which the UK became more Eurocentric. This story has often been told in economic terms—that is, in terms of the shift away from Commonwealth trade towards trade with European countries, which was a decisive factor in the decision to apply to join the EEC in the early 1960s—or in strategic terms.[28] But it is also possible to tell the story in terms of the diversion of British immigration policy that was in part a consequence of British membership. Doing so illuminates the debate about immigration during the referendum campaign in a different way than the focus on Brexit as an example of "populism".

When mass immigration to the UK began immediately after World War II, citizens of Britain's colonies had an automatic right to settle in the UK. The Nationality Act 1948 passed by the Labour government of Clement Attlee created a new category of Citizen of the United Kingdom and Colonies (or simply "British citizen"), which confirmed that citizens of British colonies had the same rights as citizens of the UK itself.[29] The Act also gave citizens of independent Commonwealth countries, including India and Pakistan, the right to settle in the UK. In the two decades following the arrival of the Empire Windrush, which brought around 500 people from the West Indies to the UK in 1948, hundreds of thousands of men and women from the Caribbean and the Indian subcontinent came to fill labour shortages—especially in the National Health Service, which had been also been created by the Labour government in 1948.

In the 1960s, as tensions increased, immigration from the "new" (that is, non-white) Commonwealth—most of whose members were now becoming independent states, even if some retained the Queen as their head of state— was restricted for the first time. The Commonwealth Immigrants Act 1962, introduced by the Conservative government, required Commonwealth citizens to apply for a work voucher in order to settle in the UK. As a large number of Asians from Kenya fled to the UK, the Labour government introduced further restrictions in 1968. The Immigration Act 1971 replaced the work vouchers that had been introduced in 1962 with work permits and in effect brought the period of large-scale primary immigration from the Commonwealth to an end.

The end of mass immigration from the Commonwealth coincided with British accession to the EC—though these two stories are rarely told together. The Immigration Act 1971 was introduced by the Conservative prime minister Edward Heath—a passionate "pro-European" who had been awarded the Charlemagne Prize in 1963—in part to clarify the rights of Commonwealth citizens in preparation for membership of the EC. When the UK joined the EC on 1 January 1973—the same day that the Immigration Act came into effect—the application of the principle of the freedom of movement of workers established in the Treaty of Rome gave citizens of EC member states priority over non-EC citizens, including Commonwealth citizens.[30] From then on, it gradually became easier for European citizens to settle in the UK—and the rights they had also gradually expanded. Meanwhile, it became harder for Commonwealth citizens to settle in the UK—and the rights they had were gradually restricted.

These post-imperial connections were part of the debate in the 1975 referendum on British membership of the EC. Then, as in 2016, both the left and right were divided around the question of Europe. But the left identified more strongly with the Commonwealth than the right—for example, in his famous speech to the Labour Party conference in 1962, Hugh Gaitskell called it "this remarkable multi-racial association, of independent nations, stretching across five continents, covering every race"—and some Labour politicians such as Barbara Castle saw entry into the EC as a betrayal of it, as we saw in chapter 3.[31] Thus the Commonwealth was "a resource for anti-colonial left" rather than a neo-colonial right.[32] Much of the British right, in fact, was critical of the Commonwealth, which it saw as a vehicle for opposition to white settler regimes in Rhodesia and South Africa and which it blamed for mass immigration to the UK.[33]

In the period between the referendum in 1975 and the end of the Cold War, the UK seemed to have found a new balance between immigration from the Commonwealth and Europe. But with the Maastricht Treaty, freedom of movement evolved as all EU citizens were given the right to live in any member state they chose. Initially, the UK remained relatively relaxed about this—so much so that the Blair government decided not to apply transitional restrictions on the number of people from central and eastern European countries who were able to come to the UK after they joined the EU in 2004.[34] The government estimated that between 5,000 and 13,000 people would come to the UK each year, but it turned out to be around 50,000 a year.[35] At the same time, the UK was also imposing further restrictions on immigration from the Commonwealth. For example, from 2003, Jamaicans were required to apply for a visa even to visit the UK.[36]

It was against this background that freedom of movement, and immigration more generally, became a salient issue in British politics in the 2000s. Unable to control immigration from the EU, Conservative governments began to take an aggressive approach to immigration from outside the EU as well as radical steps to reduce the number of people applying for asylum in the UK. In 2012, Home Secretary Theresa May sought to create a "hostile environment" for illegal immigrants.[37] It was this policy that led to the so-called Windrush scandal when it emerged that the Home Office had wrongfully sought to detain and deport at least eighty-three members of the first generation of immigrants from the Caribbean.

This history complicates the conventional narrative of Brexit in relation to immigration, which has been shaped by the tendency to see it as an example of "populism". In particular, it suggests another way of understanding the UK's withdrawal from the EU: as a kind of rebalancing of the UK's focus away from Europe—or to put it another way, its Eurocentrism—towards the rest of the world and especially the Commonwealth; or as a sudden, partial reversal of, and perhaps even a corrective to, the gradual shift in the opposite direction since the end of World War II. What this may mean is not so much a straightforward rejection of immigration or even an attempt to reduce it, as Brexit has generally been viewed, but rather as an attempt to rebalance immigration away from Europe towards the rest of the world and particularly to the Commonwealth.

In fact, since the UK left the EU, as immigration from EU member states has fallen, immigration from outside the EU and particularly from the Commonwealth has increased dramatically, leading to a large overall increase.[38] In 2021, the UK agreed to give hundreds of thousands of visas to British Overseas citizens from Hong Kong—a scheme supported by an overwhelming majority of the public.[39] These developments raise the question of whether after Brexit, regardless of the intentions of those who campaigned for it and voted for it, the UK will become a more multicultural and multiracial society. They also suggest that the question of post-Brexit Britain's relationship with its colonial past is more complex, and more open-ended, than the idea of "Empire 2.0" suggests.

## A decolonial Europe?

In a paper exploring what a decolonial project for Europe might look like—in other words what it would mean for Europe to engage more deeply and seriously with its colonial past—Gurminder Bhambra argues that scholarship on the history of European identity has tended to tell a "simple and encouraging local story" and produced a view of "Europe" as "an expression of peaceful integration and a demonstration of how a past of conflict and inequality can be overcome".[40] This story has overlooked the history and legacy of European colonialism—or, as I put it in chapter 3, it has focused on the internal lessons rather than the external lessons of European history. Instead of a Habermasian view of Europe as exemplifying an unfinished project of modernity, Bhambra proposes to see Europe in terms of "an unfinished project of decolonization".[41]

For Bhambra, the key to completing that project of decolonisation is to recognise empire as *constitutive* of European societies and states. She argues that nation states in western Europe should be understood as *imperial* states. Seeing European nation states in this way requires not simply acknowledging their imperial pasts—in other words, that they *had* empires—but going much further in understanding the way in which these empires shaped the nation states they became after decolonisation. Engaging more deeply with Europe's colonial past would involve a recognition that, as Paul Gilroy puts it, empire was a "formative experience" that shaped colonial powers in profound ways.[42] Empire was not something that "happened elsewhere".[43] Rather, it made Europe what it became.

Thinking of Europe's colonial past in this way would have consequences for its perception of itself in both internal and external terms. In particular, it would lead to a different way of thinking about the responsibility of Europe towards its former colonies. Instead of thinking in terms of aid or charity, it would think more in terms of compensation or reparations. Bhambra begins her paper with the example of Germany's approach to Namibia, a German colony from 1884 until 1915. While the Federal Republic accepted the principle of reparations in relation to the Holocaust as early as the 1950s, the "gesture of reconciliation" that it finally made to Namibia in 2021 was framed as aid, not compensation—a tendency that is common to "all countries involved in the European colonial project".[44]

Little has been written about where the EU itself might fit into such a decolonial project. Cultural studies and post-colonial studies scholars have often been critical of epistemological or methodological nationalism— that is, the tendency to understand social processes through the frame of the nation state. That has in turn sometimes led to a tendency to see a collective European approach, as a way of overcoming nationalism and thinking in more transnational terms, as being part of the solution to the problem of imperial amnesia. But it is far from clear that epistemological or methodical *regionalism*—that is, an approach in which Europe replaces the nation state as "container" or frame for analysis—is any better than epistemological or methodological nationalism.

In fact, methodological regionalism may make it even harder to foreground the connections between European countries and the rest of the world, and in particular between former colonial powers and their former colonies—and thus may make it even harder to understand western European nation states as imperial states. A European frame exacerbates the tendency among Europeans to think of their history as a "closed system"—in other words, to focus on relations with each other rather than with the rest of the world. As we have seen, it is this that has led to a tendency to remember the Holocaust while forgetting the history of European colonialism. Thus what Timothy Snyder called the "soft landing" that the EU provided after empire was actually an escape from Europe's colonial history.

In a sense, engaging more deeply with Europe's colonial past could actually be a danger to the EU. To the extent that western European countries go further in understanding their former empires as being constitutive of their own national identities, it would mostly be a project they would have to undertake individually, each with their own former colonies, rather than collectively.[45] In particular, the effect of the development of a deeper sense of western European nation states as imperial states would be to deepen the connections between each of them and their former colonies rather than with each other. Thus it would act as what in debates about European integration is often called a "centrifugal force"—one that would actually pull member states away from a European identity and have a *disintegrative* effect.

In theory, it would be possible for western European states to think of colonialism as a collective project and therefore develop a shared collective memory of it, much in the way that the Holocaust has come to be a central collective memory for the EU. This could even include other western European countries that did not themselves have extensive colonies—after all, as Bhambra points out, many citizens of countries like Ireland and Sweden took part in the colonial project as settlers.[46] But central and eastern European countries, particularly those who see themselves as the victims of Russian imperialism, would likely resist the idea that, in becoming EU member states, they also inherited responsibility for European colonialism.[47] Thus an attempt to make the memory of empire more central to the EU's identity would likely divide it between east and west.

In that sense, the EU itself may actually be part of what is preventing Europeans from engaging more deeply with their colonial past. It is not simply an accident of history that the Holocaust became a central collective memory for the EU while the memory of European colonialism was forgotten. Rather, there are structural reasons why the EU has become a vehicle for imperial amnesia that mean it is also difficult for it to correct the problem of "biased salience" and to learn and apply the external lessons of its history as well as the internal lessons. While the collective memory of the Holocaust strengthens the European project, the collective memory of European colonialism weakens it—and "pro-Europeans" therefore inevitably resist the idea of deepening engagement with it.

## Brexit as opportunity

In an influential analysis of the UK's relationship with its colonial past, Paul Gilroy has identified a state of what he calls "postcolonial melancholia". Applying the psychoanalytic approach of Alexander and Margarete Mitscherlich, who diagnosed Germany's post-war "inability to mourn" the death of Hitler, Gilroy argues that the UK never processed the consequences of its loss of empire. As Britain's imperial history became "a source of discomfort, shame and perplexity" in the post-war period, it was "diminished, denied, and then, if possible, actively forgotten".[48] Gilroy argues that this unresolved trauma produced a nation that is anxious and insecure. Yet this "postcolonial melancholia" coexists with "conviviality"—"the processes of cohabitation and interaction that have made multiculture an ordinary feature of social life in Britain's urban areas and in post-colonial cities elsewhere".[49]

During the debate about Brexit, analysts and commentators drew explicitly or implicitly on analyses by Gilroy and other cultural and post-colonial studies scholars, and sought to identify the pathology of "postcolonial melancholia" with Leavers. But Gilroy was writing at the time of the War on Terror and the war in Iraq and particularly with Blairism in mind, with its combination of "radical" centrism, "pro-Europeanism", and support for US-led military interventions, which he saw as neo-colonial.[50] As other cultural studies and post-colonial scholars have also emphasised, the legacy and memory of empire in the UK is much more complex and ubiquitous than is suggested by a straightforward equation of the phenomenon of "postcolonial melancholia" with the leave side of the Brexit argument.[51]

In fact, if Gilroy is right about a pathology of "postcolonial melancholia" in the UK, it may actually be that membership of the EU has contributed to it. His argument is that the UK never "worked through" the feelings associated with the loss of empire,[52] but membership of the EU may be part of the explanation for why. In part, this is because of the way in which the EU gave the UK, like other former colonial powers, a "soft landing" after empire. But there is also a particularly British dimension to the story. As we have seen, the end of Commonwealth immigration coincided with the UK's accession to the EC, and the way that non-white people who historically were British citizens were "reconceived and reclassified as immigrants" is connected to the UK's integration into the "European community".[53]

A European identity also exacerbates the tendency by British people to focus above all on their glorious role in liberating the continent during World War II—itself part of a longer history of "offshore balancing", that is, a foreign-policy strategy aimed at preventing the emergence of a continental European hegemon—rather than their less glorious role as a colonial power. Gilroy sees Britain's obsession with World War II as a symptom of its "postcolonial melancholia"—he writes that there is "something neurotic about Britain's continued citation of the anti-Nazi war".[54] The memory of "standing up" to Nazism in World War II is a comforting one, suggesting that the UK has been a force for good, whereas the memory of empire is a disturbing one, suggesting that the UK has played a less positive role in history.

In fact, rather than being set against each other, the two sets of histories are increasingly linked. In recent years, national institutions like the BBC and the Imperial War Museum have emphasised the hugely important contribution made by civilians and soldiers from Britain's colonies to the war effort during Britain's "finest hour". This has led to a growing awareness in the

UK that it was the British empire, rather than simply a white Britain, that "stood up" to Nazism. Thus, far from automatically leading to a nostalgia for a white Britain before mass immigration began in the 1950s, the continuous and obsessive invocation of World War II can function as a way of educating or reminding British people about the complicated history of empire.

Nevertheless, to the extent that Gilroy is right that a focus on the memory of World War II offers a kind of escape from Britain's imperial history, Brexit may be an opportunity. If the EU is a vehicle for imperial amnesia, as I have argued, Brexit may be a particular opportunity to remember the UK's colonial history in a deeper and different way. Instead of severing the links between the former colonial metropole and former colonies and re-imagining the national story as part of a history of Europe as a "closed system", as the UK has tended to do since it joined the EC in 1973, the UK can re-imagine its national story as that of the imperial state that Bhambra suggests, and deepen its understanding of how constitutive or formative empire was of what became the British nation.

Instead of thinking of itself only as being part of a European "community of fate", as the European project encouraged it to, such a post-Brexit Britain might instead, or in addition, think of itself as part of a different post-imperial network of countries. That would not mean excluding or forgetting the memory of Britain's interactions with the rest of Europe, which have also played a huge role in shaping the nation, but rather rebalancing the way the national story is imagined away from an exclusive focus on Europe. Such a rethinking of British identity and history would have extensive policy implications—especially for foreign policy. In particular, the UK would seek to develop closer relationships with its former colonies, whether that is done through the Commonwealth or on a bilateral basis.

A good place to start would be immigration policy, the focus of which has shifted away from the Commonwealth to Europe, as we have seen. It would be possible to go further in the rebalancing of British immigration policy that has taken place since Brexit—in particular, by making it easier for citizens of Britain's former colonies to come to the UK. In the 1980s, arguments for Commonwealth immigration were made in terms of the legacy of empire—a popular anti-racist slogan of the time was "We are here because you were there".[55] Although this moral-historical logic of immigration from former colonies was contested at the time, it is now widely accepted—much more than the different logic around freedom of movement. Such a policy—what might be called "post-imperial preference"—could even be thought of as a form of reparations.

Of course, it is far from inevitable that any of this will happen. In particular, it is unlikely that the British right would pursue such a vision. Rather, it would require the

British left to develop its own distinctive version of what a UK outside the EU might look like rather than simply dismissing Brexit as an inherently and necessarily right-wing project which must be either fully or partially reversed—a view that is based to a large extent on a mis-perception of the EU as a progressive or even cosmopoli-tan project. Specifically, it would require the British left to move beyond its reflex that any relationship with the UK's former colonies must be a neo-colonial one. Instead, it should see Brexit as an opportunity to make the UK become a less Eurocentric country.

# NOTES

## INTRODUCTION

1. On the idea of a repoliticisation of economic policy in Europe, see Pepijn Bergsen, Leah Downey, Max Krahé, Hans Kundnani, Manuela Moschella and Quinn Slobodian, "The economic basis of democracy in Europe. Structural economic change, inequality and the depoliticization of economic policymaking", Chatham House, September 2022, https://www.chathamhouse.org/sites/default/files/2022–09/2022–09–08-economic-basis-of-democracy-in-europe-bergsen-et-al.pdf (last accessed 31 March 2023).

2. I am thinking particularly of work done in the field of cultural studies, beginning at the Centre for Contemporary Cultural Studies at Birmingham University in the 1970s.

3. The Commission for Racial Equality has since been replaced by the Equality and Human Rights Commission, which has a broader remit.

## 1. EUROPEAN REGIONALISM

1. European Union Nobel Lecture, Oslo, 10 December 2012, https://www.nobelprize.org/prizes/peace/2012/eu/lecture/ (last accessed 31 March 2023).

2. Jürgen Habermas, "Toward a Cosmopolitan Europe",

*Journal of Democracy*, Volume 14, number 4, 2003, pp. 86–100, here p. 88. Originally published as "Euroskepsis, Markteuropa oder Europa der (Welt-)Bürger" ["Euroscepticism, a market Europe, or a Europe of (global) citizens"], *Zeit der Übergänge. Kleine Politische Schriften IX* (Frankfurt am Main: Suhrkamp, 2001), pp. 85–103.

3. See in particular Immanuel Kant, "Idea for a universal history with a cosmopolitan purpose", translated by H.B. Nisbet, in Hans Reiss (ed.), *Kant: Political Writings* (Cambridge: Cambridge University Press, 1991), pp. 41–53. ("Idee zu einer allgemeinen Geschichte in weltbürgerlicher Absicht", *Akademie Ausgabe von Immanuel Kants Gesammelten Werken*, Volume VIII, pp. 15–30.)

4. Jürgen Habermas, "Die postnationale Konstellation und die Zukunft der Demokratie", *Blätter für deutsche und internationale Politik* ["The Postnational Constellation and the Future of Democracy"], July 1998, pp. 804–817, here p. 813 (my own translation). Reproduced in Jürgen Habermas, *Die postnationale Konstellation. Politische Essays* ["The Postnational Constellation. Political Essays"] (Frankfurt am Main: Suhrkamp, 1998), pp. 91–169. For similar formulations, see "Der europäische Nationalstaat unter dem Druck der Globalisierung" ["The European nation state under the pressure of globalisation"], *Blätter für deutsche und internationale Politik*, April 1999, pp. 425–436, here p. 434; "Toward a Cosmopolitan Europe", p. 96. The term *Weltinnenpolitik* was first used by the German physicist and philosopher Carl Friedrich von Weizsäcker in 1963.

5. Jürgen Habermas, *The Crisis of the European Union: A Response* (Cambridge: Polity, 2012), p. 2.

6. Habermas, "Toward a Cosmopolitan Europe", p. 87.

7. Ulrich Beck/Edgar Grande, *Cosmopolitan Europe* (Cambridge: Polity, 2007), pp. 5, 19.

8. Ibid., p. 5, 4.

9. Ibid., p. 20.

10. He understands cosmopolitanism as "a specific way of *dealing socially with cultural difference*" in a way that avoids "hierarchical subordination, universalistic and nationalist sameness, and postmodern particularism" (emphasis in original). Ibid., p. 12.

11. Ibid., p. 14 (emphasis in original).

12. Ulrich Beck, *The Cosmopolitan Vision* (Cambridge: Polity, 2006), p. 167. Also see Peo Hansen, "Post-national Europe—without cosmopolitan guarantees", *Race & Class*, Volume 50, Issue 4, 2009, pp. 20–37.

13. On the "national self-delusion", see Beck and Grande, *Cosmopolitan Europe*, pp. 21–22. A good example of how Beck's idea of cosmopolitanism collapses into anti- or postnationalism is his claim that the European Court of Justice's assertion of the primacy of EU law over member state law represents a kind of cosmopolitan legal revolution (p. 7). Similarly, because the European Commission is the "motor of integration", he sees it as "the main institutional agency of the cosmopolitan dynamic within the EU" (p. 76). He also refers to it and the European Court of Justice as "cosmopolitan entrepreneurs" (pps. 8, 42, 138).

14. See Craig Calhoun, "Cosmopolitan Europe and European Studies", in Chris Rumford (ed.), *The Sage Handbook of European Studies* (London: Sage: 2009), pp. 637–654.

15. A number of scholars have elaborated theories of "cosmopolitan patriotism". For example, Kwame Anthony

Appiah argues that nationalism and cosmopolitanism, far from being incompatible, are "actually intertwined". Kwame Anthony Appiah, "The Importance of Elsewhere. In Defense of Cosmopolitanism", *Foreign Affairs*, March/April 1999, https://www.foreignaffairs.com/world/importance-elsewhere (last accessed 31 March 2023).

16. Some early scholars of European integration used the concept of regionalism. See for example Ernst Haas, "The challenge of regionalism", *International Organization*, Vol. 12, No. 4, October 1958, pp. 440–458.

17. There is some debate about whether Europe even qualifies as a continent. For example, J.G.A. Pocock argues that Europe is an "anomaly in our typology of continents". In particular, "Europe is not linked to Asia so much as it is an extension of it, a peninsula or subcontinent such as that of India." J.G.A. Pocock, "Some Europes in Their Histories", in Anthony Pagden (ed.), *The Idea of Europe. From Antiquity to the European Union* (Cambridge: Cambridge University Press), pp. 55–71, here pps. 57, 58.

18. Hans Kohn, *The Idea of Nationalism: A Study in Its Origins and Background* (London: Macmillan, 1944); new edition with an introduction by Craig Calhoun (New Jersey: Transaction, 2005).

19. Kohn's analysis focuses almost exclusively on the geographic West—that is, Europe and North America. The "West" refers here to the western part of what we now call the West and "East" to the eastern part of the West, in other words, central Europe.

20. Calhoun, introduction to Kohn, p. xxvi.

21. Eric Foner, *The Second Founding. How the Civil War and Reconstruction Remade the Constitution* (New York:

Norton, 2019), p. 71. On civic and racial versions of American nationalism, see also Gary Gerstle, *American Crucible. Race and Nation in the Twentieth Century* (Princeton: Princeton University Press, 2017).

22. Calhoun, introduction to Kohn, p. xl. I use the term "ethnic/cultural" instead of the narrower "ethnic" used by Kohn. This can also include identity based on religion—the distinction between ethnicity and religion is a blurry one. This is particularly the case in Europe, where racism has always been as much about culture and religion as "skin colour". For example, Paul Gilroy writes of "culture lines" as well as "color lines". Paul Gilroy, *Between Camps. Nations, Cultures, and the Allure of Race* (London: Routledge, 2004), p. 1. My use of the term "ethnic/cultural" is also informed by debates about "neo-racism"—that is, a new modality of racism based on culture rather than biology, sometimes also called "culturalist" racism or "racism without race(s)", which emerged in the post-World War II period. See Etienne Balibar, "Is There a 'Neo-Racism'?", in Etienne Balibar and Immanuel Wallerstein, *Race, Nation, Class. Ambiguous Identities* (London: Verso, 2010), pp. 17–28.

23. Calhoun, introduction to Kohn, pp. xxxiv, xli.

24. Benedict Anderson, *Imagined Communities. Reflections on the Origin and Spread of Nationalism* (London: Verso, 1983; Revised Edition 1991).

25. Ibid., p. 42.

26. Ibid., p. 36.

27. Ibid., p. 12.

28. In their work on "cosmopolitan Europe", Beck and Grande also allude to this idea of Europe as an "imagined commu-

nity", though they insist that this does not mean that they see the European project as being analogous to a national project. Beck/Grande, *Cosmopolitan Europe*, p. 7.

29. Anderson, *Imagined Communities*, p. 6.

30. Ibid., p. 6.

31. Ibid., p. 7 (emphasis in original).

32. Beck and Grande similarly refer to nations as having "limited territorial scope". In contrast, their "cosmopolitan Europe" is open-ended, with variable borders and geography. Beck/Grande, *Cosmopolitan Europe*, p. 13.

33. Hannah Arendt, "Rand School Lecture" (1948), in *Essays in Understanding, 1930–1954* (New York: Harcourt, Brace & Company, 1994), pp. 217–228, here p. 222.

34. Although they understand Europe as being cosmopolitan as we have seen, Beck and Grande do briefly discuss the possibility of a different idea of Europe that would be more analogous to nationalism but on a continental scale. They write that "a deeply unsettled Europe" could be tempted to "use the concept of civilisation to establish a pan-continental European identity that incorporates and neutralizes the antagonistic nationalisms". Beck/Grande, *Cosmopolitan Europe*, p. 129. They also refer to the idea of a "Fortress Europe" (for example p. 186).

35. Anderson, p. 141.

36. "'Le nationalisme, c'est la guerre', déclare François Mitterrand" ["'Nationalism is war', says François Mitterrand"], *Le Monde*, 19 January 1995, https://www.lemonde.fr/archives/article/1995/01/19/le-nationalisme-c-est-la-guerre-declare-francois-mitterrand_3835927_1819218.html (last accessed 31 March 2023).

37. Partha Chatterjee, *The Nation and Its Fragments: Colonial and Postcolonial Histories* (Princeton: Princeton University Press, 1993), p. 4.

38. Ibid., p. 3.

39. Amie Tsang, "E.U. Seeks Solidarity as Nations Restrict Medical Exports", *New York Times*, 7 March 2020, https://www.nytimes.com/2020/03/07/business/eu-exports-medical-equipment.html (last accessed 31 March 2023).

40. Michael Peel, Jim Brunsden and Richard Milne, "EU to curb exports of protective gear for coronavirus", *Financial Times*, 15 March 2020, https://www.ft.com/content/36fac94a-66b8-11ea-800d-da70cff6e4d3 (last accessed 31 March 2023).

41. Tweet by Ursula von der Leyen, 15 March 2020, https://twitter.com/vonderleyen/status/1239221732218744833?s=20&t=vAVoI3khYA823Xb6pEtIjA (last accessed 31 March 2023).

42. Tweet by Wolfgang Ischinger, 30 May 2020, https://twitter.com/ischinger/status/1266620632248320000?s=20&t=Nl_9TLJlRScVzJidrEVTbw (last accessed 31 March 2023).

43. See Hans Kundnani, "Le passé impensé: pour un récit critique européen" ["The unthought past: for a critical European narrative"], *Le Grand Continent*, 20 October 2021, https://legrandcontinent.eu/fr/2021/10/26/le-passe-impense-pour-un-recit-critique-europeen/ (last accessed 31 March 2023).

44. As Stuart Hall puts it, Europe tends to "disavow its historic instability and its deep interconnections with other histories." Stuart Hall, "'In but not of Europe': Europe

and its myths", *Soundings*, Issue 22, Winter, 2002–03, pp. 57–69, here p. 61, https://journals.lwbooks.co.uk/soundings/vol-2002-issue-22/article-6929/ (last accessed 31 March 2023). Reproduced in Paul Gilroy and Ruth Wilson Gilmore, *Selected Writings on Race and Difference* (New York: Duke University Press, 2021), pp. 374–385.

45. Ibid., p. 60.

46. Stuart Hall, "The West and Rest: Discourse and Power", in Stuart Hall and Bram Gieben (eds.), *Formations of Modernity* (Oxford/Cambridge: Polity Press in association with Basil Blackwell and the Open University, 1992), pp. 276–320, here p. 279.

47. Linda Colley, *Britons. Forging the Nation 1707–1837* (New Haven: Yale University Press, 1992), p. xvi.

48. German identity was also based on myths in which Rome—in the form of the Roman empire in the ancient period and the Catholic church after the Reformation—was an Other. See Herfried Münkler, *Die Deutschen und ihre Mythen* ["The Germans and Their Myths"] (Reinbek: Rowohlt, 2010).

49. Habermas, "Toward a Cosmopolitan Europe", p. 98 (emphasis in original).

50. Edgar Morin, *Penser l'Europe* ["Thinking about Europe"] (Paris: Gallimard, 1990), p. 195. Beck and Grande, on the other hand, explicitly reject the idea of Europe as a "community of fate". Beck/Grande, *Cosmopolitan Europe*, p. 132.

51. See for example Marta Lorimer, "What do they talk about when they talk about Europe? Euro-ambivalence in far right ideology", *Ethnic and Racial Studies*, Volume 44, Issue 11, 2021, pp. 2016–2033. The paper looks specifi-

cally at the literature of the Movimento Sociale Italiano (the forerunner of the Brothers of Italy, which came to power in Italy in 2022) and the Front National (now the Rassemblement National) in France.

52. Rogers Brubaker, "Between nationalism and civilization-ism: the European populist moment in comparative per-spective", *Ethnic and Racial Studies*, Volume 40, Issue 8, 2017, pp. 1191–1226.

53. Merijn Oudenampsen argues that in the case of the Netherlands, it was not simply that the centre right adopted elements of the far right's agenda, but rather a more complicated two-way process in which it is difficult to establish who is adopting whose ideas. See Merijn Oudenampsen, *The Rise of the Dutch New Right: An Intellectual History of the Rightward Shift in Dutch Politics* (London: Routledge, 2021), especially pp. 44–48.

54. On the origins and influence of white replacement the-ory, see Thomas Chatterton Williams, "The French ori-gins of 'You will not replace us'", *New Yorker*, 27 November 2017, https://www.newyorker.com/magazine/2017/12/04/the-french-origins-of-you-will-not-replace-us (last accessed 31 March 2023); Nellie Bowles, "'Replacement Theory', a Racist, Sexist Doctrine, Spreads in Far-Right Circles", *New York Times*, 18 March 2019, https://www.nytimes.com/2019/03/18/technology/replacement-the-ory.html (last accessed 31 March 2023); Nicholas Confessore and Karen Yourish, "A Fringe Conspiracy Theory, Fostered Online, Is Refashioned by the G.O.P.", *New York Times*, 15 May 2022, https://www.nytimes.com/2022/05/15/us/replacement-theory-shooting-tucker-carlson.html (last accessed 31 March 2023).

55. Norimitsu Onishi, "In France, a Racist Conspiracy Theory Edges Into the Mainstream", *New York Times*, 15 February 2022, https://www.nytimes.com/2022/02/15/world/europe/france-elections-pecresse-great-replacement.html (last accessed 31 March 2023).

56. For a similar argument, see Andrew Glencross, "The EU and the Temptation to Become a Civilizational State", *European Foreign Affairs Review*, Volume 26, Issue 2, 2021, pp. 331–350.

## 2. IDEAS OF EUROPE

1. Mark Leonard, "The meaning of pro-Europeanism—a response to Hans Kundnani", *New Statesman*, 22 February 2021, https://www.newstatesman.com/world/2021/02/meaning-pro-europeanism-response-hans-kundnani (last accessed 31 March 2023). The formulation was originally used by the Danish international relations theorist Ole Wæver in relation to the EU's understanding of security. See Ole Wæver, "European Security Identities", *Journal of Common Market Studies*, Volume 34, Issue 1, March 1996, pp. 103–132, here p. 122.

2. Luuk van Middelaar, "Europa heeft zich van zeen geschiedenis afgesneden" ["Europe has cut itself off from its history"], *NRC*, 19 May 2021, https://www.nrc.nl/nieuws/2021/05/19/europa-heeft-zich-van-zijn-geschiedenis-afgesneden-a4044010 (last accessed 31 March 2023); "L'Europe est-elle post-chrétienne?" ["Is Europe post-Christian?"], *Le Grand Continent*, 14 October 2021, https://legrandcontinent.eu/fr/2021/10/14/leurope-est-elle-post-chretienne/ (last accessed 31 March 2023).

3. Morin, *Penser l'Europe*, pp. 251–253.

4. Quoted in Shane Weller, *The Idea of Europe. A Critical History* (Cambridge: Cambridge University Press, 2021), p. 16.

5. On the use of the concept of barbarism in ancient Greece, in particular the way it was used by Aristotle and Plato to justify slavery, see Oliver Eberl, *Naturzustand und Barbarei. Begründung und Kritik staatlicher Ordnung im Zeichen des Kolonialismus* ["State of Nature and Barbarism: Justification and Criticism of State Order under the Sign of Colonialism"] (Hamburg: Hamburger Edition, 2021), pp. 77–91.

6. In *The Triumph of the West* (1985), Adam Roberts writes: "The word 'Europeans' seems to appear for the first time in an eighth-century reference to Charles Martel's victory [over Islamic forces] at Tours." Quoted in Hall and Gieben, *Formations of Modernity*, p. 289. Martel was later a resonant figure for the European far right. For example, in the 1970s, a French anti-Arab terrorist organisation calling itself the Charles Martel Group carried out attacks on Algerian targets. I would like to thank Quinn Slobodian for pointing this out to me.

7. Weller, *The Idea of Europe*, p. 24.

8. Denys Hay, *Europe: The Emergence of an Idea* (Edinburgh: Edinburgh University Press, 1957), p. 58.

9. Hay writes that "by the thirteenth century the cross had become a universal symbol from the Black Sea to the Atlantic and from the Mediterranean to the Arctic Circle". Hay, *Europe*, p. 20.

10. Hay, *Europe*, p. 109.

11. Hay, *Europe*, pps. 37, 95, 96. On the "eclipse" of Christendom by Europe, see also Mark Greengrass, *Christendom*

*Destroyed: Europe 1517–1648* (Harmondsworth: Penguin, 2014).

12. Weller, *The Idea of Europe*, p. 27. On Pius II, see also Hay, *Europe*, pp. 83–87.

13. See Hay, *Europe*, pp. 51–52; Jinty Nelson, "Charlemagne and Europe", *Journal of the British Academy*, Volume 2, 2014, pp. 125–152.

14. See Hall and Gieben (eds.), *Formations of Modernity*, p. 292. For a longer discussion of the evolution and role of Christianity in modern Europe, also see Olivier Roy, *Is Europe Christian?* (London: Hurst, 2019).

15. David Theo Goldberg, "Is Europe White? Assessing the Role of Whiteness in Europe Today", LSE online event, 15 March 2021, https://www.youtube.com/watch?v=2VKK2ukZW_s (last accessed 31 March 2023).

16. Cited in Hall, "'In but not of Europe': Europe and its myths". On the presence of people of African origin in Europe, see Olivette Otele, *African Europeans. An Untold History* (London: Hurst, 2020).

17. Columbus's four voyages were recorded in letters and dispatches written by him and others who sailed with him. Although they have not survived, scholars rely on early accounts written by authors who had access to them and quoted from them. Captain Gonzalo Fernandez de Oviedo published his official *Historia general y natural de las Indias* ["General and Natural History of the Indies"] in 1547. Columbus's son Hernando, who accompanied his father on his fourth visit, published his biography in 1571.

18. Theodore W. Allen, *The Invention of the White Race* (London: Verso, 1994/1997). Allen argues that the first recorded reference to whiteness is in 1691.

19. Histories of the concept of whiteness like Allen's tend to focus on its use in what became the United States. As far as I know, there is no equivalent history of what might be called "European whiteness"—that is, the use of the term in Europe itself and in European colonies.

20. See Jean-François Niort, *Le Code Noir. Idees recues sur un texte symbolique* ["The Code Noir. Received Ideas about a Symbolic Text"] (Paris: Le Cavalier Bleu, 2015).

21. Immanuel Wallerstein, *European Universalism. The Rhetoric of Power* (New York: New Press, 2006), p. xii.

22. Paul Gilroy, *The Black Atlantic. Modernity and Double Consciousness* (London: Verso, 1992), p. 43.

23. Sudhir Hazareesingh, *Black Spartacus. The Epic Life of Toussaint Louverture* (Harmondsworth: Penguin, 2021), pp. 4–5.

24. On Greek justifications for slavery, see Eberl, *Naturzustand und Barbarei*, pp. 77–91.

25. David Brion Davis, *The Problem of Slavery in the Age of Revolution* (Oxford: Oxford University Press, 1999), p. 263.

26. Susan Buck-Morss, *Hegel, Haiti, and Universal History* (Pittsburgh: University of Pittsburgh Press, 2009), p. 21.

27. Ibid., p. 149 (emphasis in original).

28. There is an extensive debate among Kant scholars about how to understand his racial theories—in particular, how they relate to his much-vaunted cosmopolitanism and whether his views evolved over time. See Emmanuel Chukwudi Eze, "The Idea of 'Race' in Kant's Anthropology", *Bucknell Review*, Volume 38, Issue 2, January 1995, pp. 200–241; Robert Bernasconi, "Who invented the concept of race? Kant's role in the Enlightenment

construction of race", in Robert Bernasconi (ed.), *Race* (Oxford: Blackwell, 2001); Robert Bernasconi, "Kant as an unfamiliar source of racism", in Julie K. Ward and Tommy L. Lott (eds.), *Philosophers on Race: Critical Essays* (Oxford: Blackwell, 2002), p. 145–166; Charles W. Mills, "Kant's Untermenschen", in Andrew Valls (ed.), *Race and Racism in Modern Philosophy* (Ithaca: Cornell University Press, 2005), pp. 169–193; Pauline Kleingeld, "Kant's second thoughts on race", *Philosophical Quarterly*, Volume 57, Issue 229, October 2007, pp. 573–592; Robert Bernasconi, "Kant's Third Thoughts on Race", in Stuart Elden/Eduardo Mendieta (eds.), *Reading Kant's Geography* (Albany: State University of New York Press, 2011), pp. 291–318; Charles W. Mills, "Kant and Race, Redux," *Graduate Faculty Philosophy Journal*, Volume 35, Issue 1–2, 2014, pp. 125–57. See also Eberl, *Naturzustand und Barbarei*, pp. 316–361; Robbie Shilliam, *Decolonizing Politics. An Introduction* (London: Wiley, 2021), chapter 2.

29. Immanuel Kant, "On the Different Races of Human Beings", translated by Holly Wilson and Günter Zöller, in Robert B. Louden and Günter Zöller (eds.), *The Cambridge Edition of the Works of Immanuel Kant: Anthropology, History and Education* (Cambridge: Cambridge University Press, 2007), pp. 82–97, here p. 87. ("Von den verschiedenen Racen der Menschen", *Akademie Ausgabe von Immanuel Kants Gesammelten Werken*, Volume II, pp. 427–443, here p. 432.)

30. In the original German, Kant writes that the white race "ihren vornehmsten Sitz in Europa hat" ("has it most distinguished seat in Europe"). His typology was idiosyn-

cratic: he included some people from north Africa, the Middle East and Asia in the "white race". In an unpublished note from the 1770s, Kant wrote that black and native Americans "cannot govern themselves" and "serve only for slaves" (*Akademie Ausgabe von Immanuel Kants Gesammelten Werken*, ["Academy Edition of Immanuel Kant's Collected Works"] Volume XV, p. 878.).

31. Gilroy, *The Black Atlantic*, p. 43. Charles Mills puts it slightly differently and writes of "racially restricted personhood"—he draws a distinction between humanity and personhood and suggests that while Kant accepted nonwhite people were humans, he did not see them as "persons", which he defined in a racially restricted way. Instead, they were "sub-persons", who were not morally deserving of the same freedoms and rights as white people. Mills, "Kant's Untermenschen", pp. 169–171.

32. See Sankar Muthu, *Enlightenment Against Empire* (Princeton: Princeton University Press, 2003).

33. Kenan Malik, *Not So Black and White. A History of Race from White Supremacy to Identity Politics* (London: Hurst, 2023), p. 23.

34. Kant is often seen as one of the central figures in the birth of "scientific" racism. See Mills, "Kant's Untermenschen", p. 173.

35. Cited in Peo Hansen/Stefan Jonsson, *Eurafrica. The Untold Story of European Integration and Colonialism* (London: Bloomsbury, 2014), p. 42.

36. Weller, *The Idea of Europe*, p. 146.

37. Frantz Fanon, *The Wretched of the Earth* (Harmondsworth: Penguin, 1990), p. 252.

38. Hansen/Jonsson, *Eurafrica*, p. 41.

39. José Ortega y Gasset, *Revolt of the Masses* (New York: Norton, 1957 [1932]), p. 183.

40. See Weller, *The Idea of Europe*, p. 158.

41. Ute Frevert, "Europeanizing German History", *Bulletin of the German Historical Institute*, Issue 36, Spring 2005, pp. 9–24, here p. 19, https://www.ghi-dc.org/publication/bulletin-36-spring-2005 (last accessed 31 March 2023).

42. W.E.B. Du Bois, "Of the Culture of White Folk", *Journal of Race Development*, Volume 7, Issue 4, April 1917, pp. 434–447, here p. 446.

43. Hansen/Jonsson, *Eurafrica*, pp. 54–5.

44. Richard N. Coudenhove-Kalergi, *Pan-Europe* (New York: Knopf, 1926), p. 192.

45. See Hansen/Jonsson, *Eurafrica*, pp. 26–27.

46. Richard Coudenhove-Kalergi, "Afrika", *Paneuropa*, Volume 5, Issue 2, 1929, p. 3. Coudenhove-Kalergi made it explicit that his version of the "Eurafrica" project was "in the spirit" of the Berlin conference of 1884–5 (Coudenhove-Kalergi, "Afrika", p. 17). See also Hansen/Jonsson, *Eurafrica*, p. 38. Hansen and Jonsson describe Coudenhove-Kalergi as a "fully-fledged biological racist".

47. See Hansen/Jonsson, *Eurafrica*, p. 28.

48. Weller, *The Idea of Europe*, pps. 117, 81.

49. See for example Morin, *Penser l'Europe*, p. 15.

50. Weller, *The Idea of Europe*, p. 5.

## 3. FROM COLONIAL PROJECT TO COMMUNITY OF MEMORY

1. Schuman Declaration, 9 May 1950, https://european-union.europa.eu/principles-countries-history/history-eu/

1945–59/schuman-declaration-may-1950_en        (last accessed 31 March 2023).

2. Beck and Grande, *Cosmopolitan Europe*, p. 79.

3. "The Nobel Peace Prize for 2012", 12 October 2012, https://www.nobelprize.org/prizes/peace/2012/press-release/ (last accessed 31 March 2023).

4. Timothy Snyder, "Europe's Dangerous Creation Myth", Foreign Policy, Politico, 1 May 2019, https://www.politico.eu/article/europe-creation-project-myth-history-nation-state/ (last accessed 31 March 2023). The article is based Snyder's Dahrendorf lecture at St. Antony's College, Oxford, 3 May 2019, available at https://www.youtube.com/watch?v=Dsy2assQ6uU (last accessed 31 March 2023).

5. Snyder, "Europe's Dangerous Creation Myth".

6. See Hansen/Jonsson, *Eurafrica*, p. 121.

7. Snyder, "Europe's Dangerous Creation Myth".

8. Mark Leonard, "The meaning of pro-Europeanism—a response to Hans Kundnani".

9. Italian Somaliland remained a United Nations territory under Italian administration until its independence as Somalia in 1960.

10. It retained Dutch New Guinea until it became part of Indonesia in 1963, as well as its six territories in the Caribbean. On the Dutch East Indies, see Bart Luttikhuis and A. Dirk Moses (eds.), *Colonial Counterinsurgency and Mass Violence: The Dutch Empire in Indonesia* (Abingdon: Routledge, 2014).

11. Although Algeria was officially a group of *départements*, it was not treated like *départements* in mainland France. Rather, it was governed as a colony in which rights were

differentiated along racialised lines. While European settlers and their descendants had full citizenship rights, most Muslim Algerians—so-called *indigènes*—did not.

12. Hansen/Jonsson, *Eurafrica*, p. 95.

13. On the idea of Europe as a "third force", see Ibid., pps. 72, 109, 116.

14. Ibid., p. 123; Megan Brown, *The Seventh Member State. Algeria, France, and the European Community* (Cambridge: Harvard University Press, 2022), p. 74.

15. Ibid., pp. 121–122.

16. Megan Brown, "France Can't Erase Algeria From Its History", *Foreign Policy*, 8 April 2022, https://foreignpolicy.com/2022/04/08/france-presidential-election-algeria-history-colonialism-europe-eec-africa/ (last accessed 31 March 2023).

17. Brown, *The Seventh Member State*, p. 20.

18. Hansen/Jonsson, *Eurafrica*, p. 235.

19. Ibid., pp. 157–167.

20. On Algerian oil, see Helen Thompson, *Disorder. Hard Times in the 21$^{st}$ Century* (Oxford: Oxford University Press, 2022), pp. 46–47; Brown, *The Seventh Member State*, pp. 168–169.

21. Hansen/Jonsson, *Eurafrica*, pp. 171–174.

22. Ibid., pp. 175–176.

23. Ibid., p. 238.

24. Kwame Nkrumah, Address to the Ghana National Assembly, 30 May 1961, quoted in Ibid., p. 270. On Nkrumah and the EEC see also Lindsay Aqui, "Macmillan, Nkrumah and the 1961 Application for European Economic Community Membership", *The International History Review*, Volume 39, 2017, pp. 575–591.

25. Alan Milward, *The European Rescue of the Nation-State* (Abingdon: Routledge, 1992).

26. Brown, *The Seventh Member State*, p. 3.

27. Tony Judt, *Postwar. A History of Europe since 1945* (New York: Penguin, 2005), p. 281.

28. For example, Tony Judt writes: "Charlemagne's ninth century empire corresponded with curious anticipatory precision to the original postwar Europe of the Six." Tony Judt, *A Grand Illusion? An Essay on Europe* (New York: New York University Press, 2011), p. 46.

29. Hansen/Jonsson, *Eurafrica*, p. 244.

30. Judt, *Postwar*, p. 309.

31. Paul Betts, *Ruin and Renewal. Civilising Europe after World War II* (London: Profile, 2020), p. 3.

32. Ibid., p. 86.

33. Ibid., pps. 134, 154.

34. See Michael Kimmage, *The Abandonment of the West. The History of an Idea in American Foreign Policy* (New York: Basic Books, 2020). In US foreign policy debates, Kimmage writes, the idea of the West expressed "not exactly a cultural affinity or a strategic posture but some complicated, fluid combination of these two things" (p. 13).

35. On Christian Democracy and European integration, see Wolfram Kaiser, *Christian Democracy and the Origins of European Union* (Cambridge: Cambridge University Press, 2007).

36. Rosario Forlenza, "The politics of the *Abendland*: Christian Democracy and the idea of Europe after the Second World War", *Contemporary European History*, Volume 26, Issue 2, 2017, pp. 261–286.

37. Roy, *Is Europe Christian?*, p. 1.
38. Betts, *Ruin and Renewal*, p. 135.
39. Forlenza, "The politics of the *Abendland*", p. 281.
40. Speech (extract) by Richard Nikolaus Count of Coudenhove-Kalergi, https://www.karlspreis.de/en/laureates/richard-nikolaus-graf-coudenhove-kalergi-1950/speech-extract-by-richard-nikolaus-count-of-coudenhove-kalergi (last accessed 31 March 2023).
41. Jean Monnet, *Mémoires* (Paris: Fayard, 1976), p. 339.
42. Hansen/Jonsson, *Eurafrica*, pps. 24–25, 161; Hans-Peter Schwarz, *Konrad Adenauer. Volume II: The Statesman, 1952–1967* (Oxford: Berghahn, 1995), p. 191.
43. Konrad Adenauer, *World Indivisible* (London: Allen and Unwin, 1956), cited in Betts, *Ruin and Renewal*, p. 135. Adenauer is supposed to have said that the "Asian steppe begins in Braunschweig"—that is, roughly around the border between West Germany and East Germany. "Wo Asien beginnt" ["Where Asia Begins"], *Der Spiegel*, Issue 6, 1976, https://www.spiegel.de/politik/wo-asien-beginnt-a-146217c4-0002-0001-0000-000041330760 (last accessed 31 March 2023).
44. "Protokoll der Verhandlungen des Parteitages der Sozialdemokratischen Partei Deutschlands vom 21. bis 25. Mai 1950 in Hamburg" ["Minutes of the discussions at the German Social Democratic Party Conference from 21 to 25 May 1950 in Hamburg"], p. 83, http://library.fes.de/parteitage/pdf/pt-jahr/pt-1950.pdf (last accessed 31 March 2023).
45. Christian Pineau, *Suez* (Paris: Robert Laffont, 1976), p. 71.
46. See Philip Manow, "Die soziale Marktwirtschaft als inter-

konfessioneller Kompromiss? Ein Re-Statement" ["The social market economy as an inter-confessional compromise? A restatement"], *Ethik und Gesellschaft*, Issue 1, 2010, https://www.ethik-und-gesellschaft.de/ojs/index.php/eug/article/view/1-2010-art-1/111. The Anglophile free trader Erhard opposed the creation of the EEC, which he saw as "European incest" (Hansen/Jonsson, *Eurafrica*, p. 160). He was particularly opposed to the inclusion of overseas colonies in the Treaty of Rome, which he rightly saw as an attempt to "Europeanize the costs of empire". Quinn Slobodian, *Globalists. The End of Empire and the Birth of Neoliberalism* (Cambridge, MA.: Harvard University Press, 2018), p. 194.

47. Article 3.3 of the treaty stated: "The Union shall establish an internal market. It shall work for the sustainable development of Europe based on balanced economic growth and price stability, a highly competitive social market economy, aiming at full employment and social progress, and a high level of protection and improvement of the quality of the environment. It shall promote scientific and technological advance."

48. On the emergence of the welfare state in Europe, see Judt, *Postwar*, pp. 72–77.

49. Gøsta Esping-Andersen, *The Three Worlds of Welfare Capitalism* (Princeton: Princeton University Press, 1990).

50. Jan-Werner Müller, *Contesting Democracy. Political Ideas in Twentieth-Century Europe* (New Haven: Yale University Press, 2013); Jan-Werner Müller, "Beyond Militant Democracy?" *New Left Review*, Issue 73, January/February 2012, pp. 39–47.

51. The EU's legitimacy is often seen in terms of a contrast

between "input legitimacy" (which the EU does not have) and "output legitimacy" (which the EU has through the effectiveness of its policies). My argument here is that, even during the early period of European integration, "output legitimacy" was not enough on its own to secure the support of citizens for the European project.

52. On the 1976 agreement between the EC and Algeria, see Brown, *The Seventh Member State*, pp. 235–237.

53. Brown, *The Seventh Member State*, p. 7.

54. European Council Decision of 1 October 1987, cited in *Europe Archives*, Z 207. This geographic membership criterion was later formalised in Article O ("Final Provisions") of the Maastricht Treaty (i.e. the TEU) as follows: "Any European State may apply to become a Member of the Union." Article 49 of the Treaty on European Union now states: "Any European State which respects the values referred to in Article 2 and is committed to promoting them may apply to become a member of the Union."

55. Michael Wilkinson puts it nicely: "Nothing fateful, still less emancipatory, was signified." Michael Wilkinson, *Authoritarian Liberalism and the Transformation of Modern Europe* (Oxford: Oxford University Press, 2022), p. 4.

56. Ibid., p. 4.

57. Tony Judt, *A Grand Illusion? An Essay on Europe* (New York: New York University Press, 2011), p. 16. See also Judt, *Postwar*, pp. 159–164.

58. For a good recent overview of this shift and the debates surrounding it, see Robert Saunders, *Yes to Europe! The 1975 Referendum and Seventies Britain* (Cambridge: Cambridge University Press, 2018), chapter 1.

59. Oxford Union debate, 3 June 1975.
60. Cited in Brendan Simms, *Britain's Europe. A Thousand Years of Conflict and Cooperation* (London: Allen Lane, 2006), p. 184.
61. Greenland, previously a colony, had been formally incorporated into Denmark in 1973. In 1979 it was granted greater autonomy, though it remained part of the kingdom of Denmark. Following another referendum in 1982 made possible by its new status, it left the EC in 1985. For a good discussion of Greenland's withdrawal from the EC, see Kiran Klaus Patel, *Projekt Europa. Eine kritische Geschichte* ["Project Europe: A Critical History"] (Munich: C.H. Beck, 2018), pp. 267–271.
62. Hansen, "In the Name of Europe", *Race & Class*, Volume 45, Issue 3, 2004, pp. 49–62, here p. 55. Ceula and Melilla would later become flashpoints in Europe's refugee crisis when asylum seekers attempted to break through its fortifications in order to gain access to the EU.
63. On the *Historikerstreit*, see Charles S. Maier, *The Unmasterable Past. History, Holocaust, and German National Identity* (Cambridge: Harvard University Press, 1998).
64. See Dan Diner (ed.), *Zivilisationsbruch. Denken nach Auschwitz* ["Civilisational Break. Thinking After Auschwitz"] (Frankfurt am Main: Fischer, 1988); Dan Diner, "Den Zivilisationsbruch erinnern. Über Entstehung und Geltung eines Begriffs" ["Remembering the Civilisational Break: On the Origins and Validity of a Concept"], in Heidemarie Uhl (ed.), *Zivilisatonsbruch und Gedächtniskultur. Das 20. Jahrhundert in der Erinnerung des beginnenden 21. Jahrhunderts* ["Civilisational Break and Memory Culture: The Twentieth

Century in the Memory of the Early Twenty-First Century"] (Innsbruck: StudienVerlag, 2003), pp. 17–34.

65. Wulf Kansteiner, "Transnational Holocaust Memory, Digital Culture and the End of Reception Studies", in *The Twentieth Century in European Memory. Transcultural Mediation and Reception* (Leiden: Brill, 2017), pp. 305–343, here p. 307. See also Aline Sierp and Jenny Wüstenberg, "Linking the Local and the Transnational: Rethinking Memory Politics in Europe", *Journal of Contemporary European Studies*, Volume 23, Issue 3, 2015, pp. 321–329.

66. This institutionalisation would go even further in the post-Cold War period—for example with the creation of a House of European History in Brussels, which opened in 2017. The idea was first proposed a decade earlier by European Parliament President Hans-Gert Pöttering, a German Christian Democrat, and was clearly imagined as a European version of the Haus der Geschichte (House of History) in Bonn—a particularly concrete illustration of how European memory culture followed the model set in West Germany.

67. See Jan-Werner Müller, "On European memory", in Małgorzata Pakier and Bo Stråht (eds.), *A European Memory? Contested Histories and Politics of Remembrance* (New York: Berghahn, 2010), pp. 25–37, here p. 30.

68. Aleida Assmann, "Europe: A Community of Memory?" *Bulletin of the German Historical Institute*, Issue 40, Spring 2007, pp. 11–25, here p. 13, https://www.ghi-dc.org/fileadmin/publications/Bulletin/bu40.pdf (last accessed 31 March 2023). See also Aleida Assmann, *Auf dem Weg zu einer europäischen Gedächtniskultur? Wiener Vorlesungen* ["Towards a Europe Memory Culture? Vienna Lectures"] (Vienna: Picus, 2012).

69. Judt, *Postwar*, p. 803.

70. Ibid., p. 804.

71. See Aline Sierp, "EU memory politics and Europe's forgotten colonial past", *Interventions*, Voluem 22, Issue 6, 2020 pp. 686–702. On the silence on the history of European colonialism in the House of European History, see Veronika Settele, "Including Exclusion in European Memory? Politics of Remembrance at the House of European History", *Journal of Contemporary European Studies*, Volume 23, Issue 3, 2015, pp. 405–416.

72. Avishai Margalit, *The Ethics of Memory* (Cambridge, MA: Harvard University Press, 2004), p. 80.

73. On Germany's "colonial amnesia", see Jürgen Zimmerer (ed.), *Kein Platz an der Sonne. Erinnerungsorte deutscher Kolonialgeschichte* ["No Place in the Sun: Sites of Memory of Germany's Colonial History"] (Frankfurt am Main: Campus, 2013).

74. On the particular connections between the genocide of the Herrero and Nama and the Holocaust, see Jürgen Zimmerer, *Von Windhuk nach Ausschwitz? Beiträge zum Verhältnis von Kolonialismus und Holocaust* ["From Windhoek to Auschwitz: On the Relationship Between Colonialism and the Holocaust"] (Münster: LIT, 2011).

75. David Theo Goldberg, "Racial Europeanisation", *Ethnic and Racial Studies*, Voluem 29, Issue 2, 2006, pp. 331–364, here p. 338.

76. "A Union of minorities: Seminar on Europe—Against anti-Semitism, For a Union of Diversity", Brussels, 19 February 2004, https://ec.europa.eu/commission/presscorner/detail/en/SPEECH_04_85 (last accessed 31 March 2023).

77. Ernest Renan, "Qu'est-ce qu'une nation?" ["What is a nation?"] (1882). See also Anderson, *Imagined Communities*, p. 199.

## 4. A NEW CIVILISING MISSION

1. Mark Leonard, *Why Europe Will Run the 21st Century* (London: Fourth Estate, 2005).
2. Dipesh Chakrabarty, *Provincializing Europe: Postcolonial Thought and Historical Difference* (Princeton: Princeton University Press, 2007).
3. Conversation with the author.
4. See Fritz Scharpf, *Governing in Europe. Effective and Democratic?* (Oxford: Oxford University Press, 1999).
5. Chris Bickerton, *The European Union. A Citizen's Guide*, (Harmondsworth: Penguin, 2016), p. 68.
6. Ashoka Mody, *EuroTragedy. A Drama in Nine Acts* (New York: Oxford University Press, 2018), p. 160.
7. Judt, *Postwar*, p. 715.
8. Declaration on European Identity, 14 December 1973.
9. Presidency conclusions, Copenhagen European Council, 21–22 June 1993.
10. In 1992, for example, a European Commission report said: "For the new democracies, Europe remains a powerful idea, signifying the fundamental values and aspirations which their peoples kept alive during long years of oppression." European Commission report on Europe and the Challenge of Enlargement, 24 June 1992.
11. Wilkinson, *Authoritarian Liberalism and the Transformation of Modern Europe*, p. 143.
12. Ibid., p. 144.
13. Lisbet Hooghe and Gary Marks, "A Postfunctionalist

Theory of European Integration: From Permissive Consensus to Constraining Dissensus", *British Journal of Political Science*, Voluem 39, Issue 1, 2009, pp. 1–23.

14. See Peter Mair, "Political Opposition and the European Union", *Government and Opposition*, Volume 42, Issue 1, 2017, pp. 1–17.

15. Larry Wolff, *Inventing Eastern Europe. The Map of Civilization on the Mind of the Enlightenment* (Palo Alto: Stanford University Press, 1994).

16. Ibid., p. 5.

17. Ibid., p. 7.

18. In some cases it was the same travellers like Captain John Smith, who wrote about Russia and later became famous for his role in establishing the settlement in Virginia. See ibid., pp. 10–11.

19. Ibid., p. 9.

20. See Hilary Appel and Mitchell A. Orenstein, *From Triumph to Crisis: Neoliberal Economic Reform in Postcommunist Countries* (Cambridge : Cambridge University Press, 2018); David Ost, *The Defeat of Solidarity. Anger and Politics in Postcommunist Europe* (Ithaca: Cornell University Press, 2007); Philipp Ther, *Europe since 1989: A History* (Princeton: Princeton University Press, 2016).

21. Ivan Krastev, "The Strange Death of the Liberal Consensus", *Journal of Democracy*; Volume 18, Issue 4, October 2007, pp. 56–63, here pp. 58–59; Bickerton, *The European Union: A Citizen's Guide*, p. 170.

22. Krastev, "The Strange Death of the Liberal Consensus", p 59.

23. Jan Zielonka, "Europe's new civilising missions: the EU's normative power discourse", *Journal of Political Ideologies*, Volume 18, Issue 1, 2013, pp. 35–55, here p. 35.

24. Ibid., p. 40.
25. Ibid., p. 36.
26. Ibid., p. 38.
27. Ibid., p. 43.
28. See Ivan Krastev and Stephen Holmes, *The Light That Failed. A Reckoning* (London: Allen Lane, 2019), especially pp. 7–13.
29. Olli Rehn, "Values define Europe, not borders", *Financial Times*, 3 January 2005, https://www.ft.com/content/c84dbbac-5dbc-11d9-ac01–00000e2511c8 (last accessed 31 March 2023).
30. On perceptions of Turkey within the EU and the way Europe is constructed in the discourse of Turkish accession to the EU, see Senem Aydın-Düzgit, *Constructions of European Identity. Debates and Discourses on Turkey and the EU* (Basingstoke: Palgrave, 2012).
31. "Pour ou contre l'adhésion de la Turquie à l'Union européenne" ["For or against Turkish accession to the European Union"], *Le Monde*, 8 November 2002, https://www.lemonde.fr/europe/article/2002/11/08/pour-ou-contre-l-adhesion-de-la-turquie-a-l-union-europeenne_297386_3214.html (last accessed 31 March 2023).
32. Alain Gresh, "Malevolent fantasy of Islam", *Le Monde Diplomatique*, August 2005, https://mondediplo.com/2005/08/16lewis (last accessed 31 March 2023); David Gow and Ewen MacAskill, "Turkish accession could spell end of EU, says commissioner", *The Guardian*, 8 September 2004, https://www.theguardian.com/world/2004/sep/08/turkey.eu (last accessed 31 March 2023). On Bolkestein's role in Dutch politics, see Merijn

Oudenampsen, *The Rise of the Dutch New Right: An Intellectual History of the Rightward Shift in Dutch Politics* (London: Routledge, 2021). Perry Anderson goes so far as to describe Bolkestein, with his "hardline combination of free market economics and anti-immigrant sentiment", as "the Dutch version of Enoch Powell". Perry Anderson, *Ever Closer Union? Europe in the West* (London: Verso, 2021), p. 81.

33. Rehn, "Values define Europe, not borders".

34. On the concepts of "de-bordering" and "re-bordering", see Frank Schimmelfennig, "Rebordering Europe: external boundaries and integration in the European Union", *Journal of European Public Policy*, Volume 28, Issue 3, 2001, pp. 311–330.

35. Branko Milanovic, "Democracy of convenience, not of choice: why is Eastern Europe different", Global Inequality, 23 December 2017, http://glineq.blogspot.com/2017/12/democracy-of-convenience-not-of-choice.html (last accessed 31 March 2023).

36. James Mark and Quinn Slobodian, "Eastern Europe in the Global History of Decolonization", in Martin Thomas and Andrew Thompson, *The Oxford Handbook of the Ends of Empire* (Oxford: Oxford University Press, 2019), pp. 351–372, here p. 352.

37. Ibid., p. 353. On the way that the "Eurafrica" project was meant to offer central and eastern Europeans "a share in the colonial experience" and thus correct a perceived historical injustice, see Benjamin J. Thorpe, "Eurafrica: A Pan-European Vehicle for Central European Colonialism (1923–1939)", *European Review*, Volume 26, Issue 3, 2018, pp. 503–513.

38. See Maria Mälksoo, "The Memory Politics of Becoming European: The East European Subalterns and the Collective Memory of Europe", *European Journal of International Relations*, Volume 15, Issue 4, 2009, pp. 653–680. In 1995, the European Parliament had agreed to make 27 January Holocaust Memorial Day. In 2009, it also agreed to make 23 August a European Day of Remembrance for Victims of all Totalitarian and Authoritarian Regimes.

39. Beck and Grande, *Cosmopolitan Europe*, pps. 9, 132.

40. Milan Kundera, "The Tragedy of Central Europe", *New York Review of Books*, 26 April 1984, pp. 33–38, here p. 33. Originally published as "Un Occident kidnappé ou la tragédie de l'Europe centrale", *Le Débat*, Issue 5, 1983, pp. 3–23.

41. Perry Anderson wrote perceptively that central Europe was "a space proclaiming itself centre and border at the same time". Perry Anderson, "The Europe to come", *London Review of Books*, 25 January 1996.

42. Ian Black, "Christianity bedevils talk on EU treaty", *The Guardian*, 24 May 2004, https://www.theguardian.com/world/2004/may/25/eu.religion (last accessed 31 March 2023).

43. See also Talal Asad, "Muslims and European Identity: Can Europe represent Islam?", in Anthony Pagden (ed.), *The Idea of Europe: From Antiquity to the European Union* (Cambridge: Cambridge University Press, 2002), p. 219.

44. Wolff, *Investing Eastern Europe*, p. 15.

45. József Böröcz, "'Eurowhite' Conceit, 'Dirty White' Ressentiment: 'Race' in Europe", *Sociological Forum*, Volume 36, Issue 4, December 2021, pp. 1116–1134, here p. 1116.

46. Ibid., p. 1129.

47. Wilkinson, *Authoritarian Liberalism and the Transformation of Modern Europe*, p. 159.

48. François Duchêne, "The European Community and the Uncertainties of Interdependence", in Max Kohnstamm and Wolfgang Hager (eds.), *A Nation Writ Large? Foreign Policy Problems before the European Community* (Basingstoke: Macmillan, 1973). See also Jan Orbie, "Civilian Power Europe: Review of the Original and Current Debates", *Cooperation and Conflict*, Volime 41, Issue 1, March 2006, pp. 123–128.

49. Norbert Elias, *The Civilizing Process* (Oxford: Blackwell, 1994). Originally published in German in 1939 as *Über den Prozeß der Zivilisation*.

50. Ian Manners, "Normative Power Europe: A Contradiction in Terms?", *Journal of Common Market Studies*, Volume 40, Issue 2, 2002, pp. 235–258.

51. On "normative power" and the lack of self-reflexivity, see Thomas Diez, "Constructing the Self and Changing Others: Reconsidering 'Normative Power Europe'", *Millenium: Journal of International Politics*, Volume 33, Issue 3, 2016, pp. 613–636.

52. See for example Robert Kagan, *Of Paradise and Power. America and Europe in the New World Order* (New York: Knopf, 2003). Kagan writes: "Europe is turning away from power, or to put it a little differently, it is moving beyond power into a self-contained world of laws and rules and transnational negotiation and cooperation. It is entering a post-historical paradise of peace and relative prosperity, the realization of Kant's 'Perpetual Peace.' The United States, meanwhile, remains mired in history, exer-

cising power in the anarchic Hobbesian world where international laws and rules are unreliable and where true security and the defense and promotion of a liberal order still depend on the possession and use of military might. That is why on major strategic and international questions today, Americans are from Mars and Europeans are from Venus: They agree on little and understand one another less and less." (p. 1).

53. Jürgen Habermas and Jacques Derrida, "Unsere Erneuerung. Nach dem Krieg: Die Wiedergeburt Europas" ["Our Renewal. After the War: The rebirth of Europe"], *Frankfurter Allgemeine Zeitung*, 31 May 2003.

54. Jan-Werner Müller, "European intellectuals need to quit playing the 'identity game'", Politico, 9 July 2003, https://www.politico.eu/article/europes-intellectuals-need-to-quit-playing-the-identity-game/ (last accessed 31 March 2023). In another typical example of this perceived contrast between Europe and the United States, which also illustrates the idealisation of the EU and lack of self-reflexivity and the confusion of Europe with the EU, Beck and Grande write: "Although the United States possesses the military capabilities, it lacks moral and legitimating power; the Europeans are weak, but they possess the legitimating power and morality and law." Beck/Grande, *Cosmopolitan Europe*, p. 255.

## 5. THE CIVILISATIONAL TURN IN THE EUROPEAN PROJECT

1. Jean-Claude Juncker Interview: "The Demons Haven't Been Banished", Spiegel Online, 11 March 2013, available at http://www.spiegel.de/international/europe/spiegel-

interview-with-luxembourg-prime-minister-juncker-a-888021.html (last accessed 31 March 2023).

2. A particularly significant moment in this respect was Chancellor Angela Merkel's insistence on including the IMF in the eurozone's response to the crisis. According to Greek finance minister George Papaconstantinou, French president Nicolas Sarkozy told him: "Forget the IMF. The IMF is not for Europe. It's for Africa—it's for Burkina Faso!". Quoted in Adam Tooze, *Crashed. How a Decade of Financial Crises Changed the World* (London: Allen Lane, 2018), p. 333.

3. See for example Ivan Krastev and Mark Leonard, "New World Order: The balance of soft power and the rise of the herbivorous powers", European Council on Foreign Relations, 2007, https://ecfr.eu/wp-content/uploads/ECFR-01_NEW_WORLD_ORDER_-_THE_BALANCE_OF_SOFT_POWER.pdf (last accessed 31 March 2023).

4. European Council on Foreign Relations, European Foreign Policy Scorecard 2012, January 2012, p. 11, https://ecfr.eu/archive/page/-/ECFR_SCORECARD_2012_WEB.pdf (last accessed 31 March 2023). I was one of the co-authors of this report.

5. Kim Willsher, "French minister defends offer of security forces to Tunisia", *The Guardian*, 18 January 2011, https://www.theguardian.com/world/2011/jan/18/french-minister-tunisia-offer (last accessed 31 March 2023).

6. Catherine Ashton, "The EU wants 'deep democracy' to take root in Tunisia and Egypt", *The Guardian*, 4 February 2011, https://www.theguardian.com/commentisfree/2011/feb/04/egypt-tunisia-eu-deep-democracy (last accessed 31 March 2023).

7. The fear of competition in agricultural products had long shaped relations with North Africa, including in the negotiations about the initial inclusion of Algeria in the EEC. In particular, Italy had feared that EEC agricultural subsidies would be directed away from its own *mezzogiorno* to Algeria. See Brown, *The Seventh Member State*, pp. 158–163.

8. See Mark Leonard and Nicu Popescu, "A Power Audit of EU-Russia Relations, European Council on Foreign Relations", November 2007, https://ecfr.eu/wp-content/uploads/ECFR-02_A_POWER_AUDIT_OF_EU-RUSSIA_RELATIONS.pdf (last accessed 31 March 2023). In 2007, Putin gave a speech at the Munich Security Conference which is often seen as the beginning of a more aggressive Russian approach to NATO and the EU.

9. "The Merkel Plan", *The Economist*, 15 June 2013, https://www.economist.com/news/special-report/21579144-germanys-vision-europe-all-about-making-continent-more-competitive-merkel (last accessed 31 March 2023).

10. Adam Tooze, "A Modern Greek Tragedy", *New York Review of Books*, 8 March 2018, http://www.nybooks.com/articles/2018/03/08/yanis-varoufakis-modern-greek-tragedy/ (last accessed 31 March 2023).

11. See Oliver Nachtwey, *Germany's Hidden Crisis. Social Decline in the Heart of Europe* (London: Verso, 2018). Originally published in German as *Die Abstiegsgesellschaft: Über das Aufbegehren in der regressiven Moderne* (Frankfurt am Main: Suhrkamp, 2016).

12. Hans Kundnani, "Europe and the Return of History", *Journal of Modern European History*, Volume 11, Issue 3, August 2013, pp. 279–286.

13. See Wade Jacoby and Jonathan Hopkin, "From lever to club? Conditionality in the European Union during the financial crisis", *Journal of European Public Policy*, Volume 27, Issue 8, pp. 1157–1177.

14. See Hans Kundnani, "Discipline and Punish", *Berlin Policy Journal*, 27 April 2018, https://berlinpolicyjournal.com/ discipline-and-punish/ (last accessed 31 March 2023).

15. In July 2015, after the German finance minister Wolfgang Schäuble had proposed to place €50 billion of Greek assets in a trust in Luxembourg before being privatised and to "temporarily" eject Greece from the eurozone if it did not agree to the creditors' terms, the Italian economist Luigi Zingales wrote: "If Europe is nothing but a bad version of the IMF, what is left of the European integration project?" Luigi Zingales, "The euro lives for another day, this European project is dead forever", Europa o no, 14 July 2015, https://europaono.com/2015/07/14/ zingales-euro-lives-another-day-this-european-project-dead-forever-euro-sopravvive-altro-giorno-attuale-progetto-integrazione-europea-morto-per-sempre/ (last accessed 31 March 2023).

16. See Claus Offe, *Europe Entrapped* (Cambridge: Polity, 2016).

17. Konrad Popławski, "The Role of Central Europe in the German Economy. The Political Consequences", Centre for Eastern Studies, May 2016, p. 6, https://www.osw.waw.pl/en/publikacje/osw-report/2016–05–16/role-central-europe-german-economy-political-consequences (last accessed 31 March 2023).

18. See Hans Kundnani, *The Paradox of German Power* (London: Hurst, 2014), pps. 74–75, 111.

19. See Henry Foy, "Slovakia rules out further financial aid for Greece", *Financial Times*, 19 February 2015, https://www.ft.com/content/692bfc12-b831–11e4–86bb-00144feab7de (last accessed 31 March 2023). Slovak finance minister Peter Kažimír was particularly vocal on Twitter. See Gabrielle Steinhauser, Liis Kängsepp and Juris Kaža, "Greece's Small but Mighty Critics in Eastern Europe Start to Vent", *Wall Street Journal*, 11 July 2015, https://www.wsj.com/articles/greeces-small-but-mighty-critics-in-eastern-europe-start-to-vent-1436607216 (last accessed 31 March 2023).

20. Slovak prime minister Robert Fico would later go so far as to declare that he would not accept "a single Muslim" under such a scheme. Henry Foy, "Slovakia election: PM uses migrant fears to boost poll support", 3 March 2016, *Financial Times*, https://www.ft.com/content/f3c6a6f8-e11e-11e5–8d9b-e88a2a889797 (last accessed 31 March 2023).

21. Thomas Kirchner, "Orbán: Die Flüchtlingskrise ist ein deutsches Problem", ["Orbán: The refugee crisis is a German problem"], *Süddeutsche Zeitung*, 3 September 2015, https://www.sueddeutsche.de/politik/europa-orban-die-fluechtlingskrise-ist-ein-deutsches-problem-1.2633037 (last accessed 31 March 2023).

22. "Orbán wirft Merkel 'moralischen Imperialismus' vor" ["Orbán accuses Merkel of 'moral imperialism'"], *Süddeutsche Zeitung*, 23 September 2015, https://www.sueddeutsche.de/bayern/csu-klausur-orban-wirft-merkel-moralischen-imperialismus-vor-1.2661549 (last accessed 31 March 2023).

23. "Prime Minister Viktor Orbán's Speech at the 25th

Bálványos Summer Free University and Student Camp", 30 July 2014, https://2015–2019.kormany.hu/en/the-prime-minister/the-prime-minister-s-speeches/prime-minister-viktor-orban-s-speech-at-the-25th-balvanyos-summer-free-university-and-student-camp (last accessed 31 March 2023).

24. Esther King, "Emmanuel Macron: 'Europe is not a super-market'", Politico, 22 June 2017, https://www.politico.eu/article/emmanuel-macron-europe-is-not-a-supermar-ket/ (last accessed 31 March 2023).

25. See Didier Fassin, "Sure looks a lot like conservatism", *London Review of Books*, 5 July 2018, https://www.lrb.co.uk/the-paper/v40/n13/didier-fassin/sure-looks-a-lot-like-conservatism (last accessed 31 March 2023).

26. See for example "Britain is part of 'arc of instability' around the EU, chairman says", Reuters, 28 September 2020, https://www.reuters.com/article/uk-britain-eu-michel-idUKKBN26J2BH (last accessed 31 March 2023).

27. On "European sovereignty", see Hans Kundnani, "Europe's sovereignty conundrum", *Berlin Policy Journal*, 13 May 2020, https://berlinpolicyjournal.com/europes-sover-eignty-conundrum/ (last accessed 31 March 2023).

28. See for example Carl Bildt, "Trump's decision to blow up the Iran deal is a massive attack on Europe", *Washington Post*, 12 May 2018, https://www.washing-tonpost.com/news/global-opinions/ wp/2018/05/12/trumps-decision-to-blow-up-the-iran-deal-is-a-massive-attack-on-europe/?utm_term=.ca8f6e239282 (last accessed 31 March 2023).

29. Emily Schultheis, "Viktor Orbán: Hungary doesn't want

'Muslim invaders'", Politico, 8 January 2018, https://
www.politico.eu/article/viktor-orban-hungary-doesnt-
want-muslim-invaders/ (last accessed 31 March 2023).

30. On the Five Star Movement as a "techno-populist" party,
see Chris Bickerton and Carlo Invernizzi Accetti,
"'Techno-populism' as a new party family: the case of the
Five Star Movement and Podemos", *Contemporary Italian
Politics*, Volume 10, Issue 2, 2018, pp. 132–50.

31. Ceylan Yeginsu, "Dutch Leader Takes Trump-like Turn
in Face of Hard-Right Challenge", *New York Times*,
24 January 2017, https://www.nytimes.com/2017/
01/24/world/europe/mark-rutte-netherlands-muslim-
immigrants-trump.html (last accessed 31 March 2023);
Simon Schuster, "Austria's Young Chancellor Sebastian
Kurz Is Bringing the Far-Right Into the Mainstream",
*Time*, 29 November 2018, https://time.com/5466497/
sebastian-kurz/ (last accessed 31 March 2023).

32. On Bolkestein and Huntington, see Oudenampsen, *The
Rise of the Dutch New Right*, pp. 82–85.

33. The EPP's *Spitzenkandidat* was the Bavarian Christian
Democrat Manfred Weber, whom the liberals and social-
ists in the European Parliament rejected because he had
long protected Orbán. EPP members in turn rejected the
socialist group's *Spitzenkandidat*, the Dutch Commissioner Frans Timmermanns, who was responsible for rule
of law issues and had clashed with the Hungarian and
Polish governments. 383 members of the European
Parliament voted for von der Leyen, 327 voted against
her, and 22 abstained—a relatively narrow majority. PiS
had 26 seats in the European Parliament and Fidesz 13.
See R. Daniel Kelemen, "This is how Europe got its new

president. It was a difficult and controversial process", *Washington Post*, 27 July 2019, https://www.washington-post.com/politics/2019/07/17/this-is-how-europe-got-its-new-president-it-wasnt-pretty-process/ (last accessed 31 March 2023).

34. Speech by Ursula von der Leyen, 29 November 2019, https://ec.europa.eu/commission/presscorner/detail/en/SPEECH_19_6408 (last accessed 31 March 2023).

35. See Hans Kundnani, "Europe's geopolitical confusion", *Internationale Politik Quarterly*, January 2023, https://ip-quarterly.com/en/europes-geopolitical-confusion (last accessed 31 March 2023).

36. Matina Stevis-Gridneff, "'Protecting Our European Way of Life'? Outrage Follows New E.U. Role", *New York Times*, 12 September 2019, https://www.nytimes.com/2019/09/12/world/europe/eu-ursula-von-der-leyen-migration.html (last accessed 31 March 2023).

37. Speech by Lionel Jospin on "The Future of an Enlarged Europe", 28 May 2001. See also the discussion of this speech by Jürgen Habermas in "Why Europe Needs a Constitution", *New Left Review*, September/October 2011. See also Judt, *Postwar*, Chapter XXIV.

38. Roderick Parkes, "The Siege Mentality. How Fear of Migration Explains the EU's approach to Libya", Foreign Policy Research Institute/Heinrich Böll Stiftung, November 2020, https://www.fpri.org/article/2020/12/the-siege-mentality-how-fear-of-migration-explains-the-eus-approach-to-libya/ (last accessed 31 March 2023).

39. "Uniforms of the European Border and Coast Guard standing corps", Frontex, 2 February 2021, https://fron-tex.europa.eu/media-centre/multimedia/videos/uni-

forms-of-the-european-border-and-coast-guard-standing-corps-Fv4XEx (last accessed 31 March 2023); Lorenzo Todo, "Revealed: 2,000 refugee deaths linked to illegal EU pushbacks", *The Guardian*, 5 May 2021, https://www.theguardian.com/global-development/2021/may/05/revealed-2000-refugee-deaths-linked-to-eu-pushbacks (last accessed 31 March 2023); Katy Fallon, "Revealed: EU border agency involved in hundreds of refugee pushbacks", *The Guardian*, 28 April 2022, https://www.theguardian.com/global-development/2022/apr/28/revealed-eu-border-agency-involved-in-hundreds-of-refugee-pushbacks (last accessed 31 March 2023); Katy Fallon, "EU border agency accused of serious rights violations in leaked report", *The Guardian*, 14 October 2022, https://www.theguardian.com/global-development/2022/oct/14/eu-border-agency-frontex-human-rights-violations-report (last accessed 31 March 2023)

40. "Discours du Président de la République Emmanuel Macron à la conférence des ambassadeurs et des ambassadrices de 2019" ["Speech by President Emmanuel Macron to the conference of ambassadors"], 27 August 2019, https://www.elysee.fr/emmanuel-macron/2019/08/27/discours-du-president-de-la-republique-a-la-conference-des-ambassadeurs-1 (last accessed 31 March 2023).

41. "Regierungserklärung von Bundeskanzler Olaf Scholz am 27. Februar 2022" ["Speech by Chancellor Olaf Scholz on 27 February 2022"], https://www.bundesregierung.de/breg-de/suche/regierungserklaerung-von-bundeskanzler-olaf-scholz-am-27-februar-2022–2008356 (last accessed 31 March 2023).

42. For example, a month after the war began, Scholz said in an interview that what scared him was how Putin thought in such geopolitical terms because this represented a rejection of the European "peace order". In other words, while others were urging the EU to become more "geopolitical", he thought "geopolitics" remained something to be rejected rather than aspired to. "Bundeskanzler Olaf Scholz zu Gast bei Anne Will" ["Chancellor Olaf Scholz on the Anne Will show"], 27 March 2022, https://das-erste.ndr.de/annewill/videos/Bundeskanzler-Olaf-Scholz-zu-Gast-bei-ANNE-WILL,annewill7452.html (last accessed 31 March 2023).

43. Meabh McMahon, "Ukraine is one of us and we want them in EU, Ursula von der Leyen tells Euronews", Euronews, 27 February 2022, https://www.euronews.com/2022/02/27/ukraine-is-one-of-us-and-we-want-them-in-eu-ursula-von-der-leyen-tells-euronews (last accessed 31 March 2023).

44. On the Azov Battalion, see Shaun Walker, "Azov fighters are Ukraine's greatest weapon and may be its greatest threat", *The Guardian*, 10 September 2014, https://www.theguardian.com/world/2014/sep/10/azov-far-right-fighters-ukraine-neo-nazis (last accessed 31 March 2023); Simon Shuster and Billy Perigo, "Like, Share, Recruit: How a White-Supremacist Militia Uses Facebook to Radicalize and Train New Members", *Time*, 7 January 2021, https://time.com/5926750/azov-far-right-movement-facebook/ (last accessed 31 March 2023). See also Andreas Umland, "Irregular Militias and Radical Nationalism in Post-Euromaydan Ukraine: The Prehistory and Emergence of the 'Azov' Battalion in 2014", *Terrorism and Political Violence*, Volume 31, Issue 1, 2019, pp. 105–131.

45. Deputy chief prosecutor David Sakvarelidze, interview with BBC World, 27 February 2022.

46. See Emily Venturi and Anna Iasmi Vallianatou, "Ukraine exposes Europe's double standards for refugees", Chatham House, 30 March 2022, https://www.chathamhouse. org/2022/03/ukraine-exposes-europes-double-stan-dards-refugees (last accessed 31 March 2023).

47. Even as it welcomed Ukrainians, the Polish government continued to push back asylum seekers from the Middle East on the border with Belarus. See Lorenzo Tondo, "Embraced or pushed back: on the Polish border, sadly, not all refugees are welcome", *The Guardian*, 4 March 2022, https://www.theguardian.com/global-develop-ment/commentisfree/2022/mar/04/embraced-or-pushed-back-on-the-polish-border-sadly-not-all-refugees-are-welcome (last accessed 31 March 2023).

48. Speech by HR/VP Josep Borrell at opening of the Festival d'Europa, Florence, 5 May 2022, https://www.eeas. europa.eu/eeas/speech-hrvp-josep-borrell-opening-fes-tival-d'europa-firenze-5-may-2022_en (last accessed 31 March 2023).

49. Florence Gaub on the Markus Lanz show, ZDF, 12 April 2022, https://www.youtube.com/watch?v=QFP3KIY IBWY (last accessed 31 March 2023). See also Gaub's Twitter thread, 13 April 2022, https://twitter.com/flor-encegaub/status/1514152917556727813?lang=en-GB (last accessed 31 March 2023).

50. See for example Sylvie Kaufmann, "War in Ukraine has shaken the EU's power dynamics", *Financial Times*, 30 August 2022, https://www.ft.com/content/2206a011-8769-4205-a5d1-f98492cb73b5 (last accessed 31 March

2023); "The Remaking of Europe", The Rachman Review Podcast, *Financial Times*, 29 September 2022, https://www.ft.com/content/e4dc80c0-ab3a-47dd-a9ee-265d715bdc13 (last accessed 31 March 2023).

51. Josep Borrell, "Putin's War Has Given Birth to Geopolitical Europe", European External Action Service, 3 March 2022, https://www.eeas.europa.eu/eeas/putins-war-has-given-birth-geopolitical-europe_en (last accessed 31 March 2023).

## 6. BREXIT AND IMPERIAL AMNESIA

1. Robert Saunders, "Brexit and Empire: 'Global Britain' and the Myth of Imperial Nostalgia", *The Journal of Imperial and Commonwealth History*, Volume 48, Issue 6, 2020, pp. 1–35, here p. 26.

2. Saunders, "Brexit and Empire: 'Global Britain' and the Myth of Imperial Nostalgia", p. 15 (emphasis in original). Certainly, the countries which right-wing Leavers saw as models for the UK were not imperial powers but small, affluent countries like Singapore and Switzerland.

3. Ibid., pps. 3, 21–25.

4. Ibid., p. 4.

5. Ibid., p. 8.

6. Ibid., p. 7. See also Saunders, *Yes to Europe!*, pp. 263–265.

7. See for example Ronald Inglehart and Pippa Norris, *Cultural Backlash: Trump, Brexit, and Authoritarian Populism* (Cambridge: Cambridge University Press, 2019).

8. On the role of racial resentment in the election of Trump, see John Sides, Michael Tesler and Lynn Vavreck, *Identity Crisis: The 2016 Presidential Campaign and the Battle for the Meaning of America* (Princeton: Princeton University Press, 2018), pps. 30–31, 175–179.

9. On the United States, see the extensive work of David Autor, David Dorn, Gordon Hanson and Kaveh Majlesi. On the UK, see for example Italo Cantalone and Piero Stanig, "Global Competition and Brexit", *American Political Science Review*, Volume 11, Issue 2, 2019, pp. 201–208.

10. Helen Thompson, "Inevitability and contingency: The political economy of Brexit", *The British Journal of Politics and International Relations*, Vol. 19, No. 3, 2017, pp. 434–449, here p. 446.

11. Ibid., p. 434.

12. "Ethnic minority" refers here to the UK's population of people of African, Asian and Caribbean origin, sometimes also referred to as "black and Asian" or "black, Asian and minority ethnic" (BAME).

13. 31 per cent of ethnic minority voters voted to leave the EU, compared to 69 per cent who voted to remain. Ethnic minority voters divided along similar class, educational, generational, and regional lines as white voters, but turnout was significantly lower among ethnic minorities than among the white population, suggesting a general relative indifference towards the question of membership of the EU. See Ipsos, "How Britain voted in the 2016 EU referendum", 5 September 2016, https://www.ipsos.com/en-uk/how-britain-voted-2016-eu-referendum (last accessed 31 March 2023). Saunders suggests that this means that those who disliked the EU stayed home instead of voting for Leave. Saunders, "Brexit and Empire: 'Global Britain' and the Myth of Imperial Nostalgia", p. 20.

14. Neema Begum, "Minority ethnic attitudes and the 2016 EU referendum", UK in a Changing Europe, 6 February

2018, http://ukandeu.ac.uk/minority-ethnic-attitudes-and-the-2016-eu-referendum/ (last accessed 31 March 2023).

15. Neema Begum, "British democracy and ethnic minority voters", UK in a Changing Europe, 8 July 2020, https://ukandeu.ac.uk/neema-begum-british-democracy-and-ethnic-minority-voters/ (last accessed 31 March 2023).

16. Begum, "Minority ethnic attitudes and the 2016 EU referendum". A 2015 report on ethnic minority views of immigration found similar views of the EU: "Some view Europe in explicitly ethnic or racial terms, identifying 'Fortress Europe' as a way of keeping out non-white immigration while allowing significant levels of European migration". Omar Khan and Debbie Weekes-Bernard, "This is Still About Us. Why Ethnic Minorities See Immigration Differently", Runnymede Trust, December 2015, https://www.runnymedetrust.org/publications/this-is-still-about-us-why-ethnic-minorities-see-immigration-differently (last accessed 31 March 2023), p. 4.

17. Neema Begum, "Is being European a white identity? Brussels needs deep reflection in the wake of the Black Lives Matter movement", *The Conversation*, 8 July 2020, https://theconversation.com/is-being-european-a-white-identity-brussels-needs-deep-reflection-in-the-wake-of-the-black-lives-matter-movement-141902 (last accessed 31 March 2023).

18. "What Does Brexit Mean for Black and Asian Britain?", discussion at the Mile End Institute, Queen Mary University of London, 28 November 2018, https://www.youtube.com/watch?v=19jlfIoz4s4 (last accessed 31 March 2023).

19. Begum, "Is being European a white identity?".

20. Michaela Benson and Chantelle Lewis, "Brexit, British People of Colour in the EU-27 and everyday racism in Britain and Europe", *Ethnic and Racial Studies*, Volume 42, Issue 13, 2019, pp. 2211–2228.

21. Ibid., p. 2221.

22. Ibid., p. 2223.

23. "Sol Campbell warns fans to stay away from Euro 2012", BBC, 28 May 2012, https://www.bbc.co.uk/news/uk-18192375 (last accessed 31 March 2023); John Ashdown, "Theo Walcott's family to miss Euro 2012 for fear of racist attacks", *The Guardian*, 17 May 2012, https://www.theguardian.com/football/2012/may/17/theo-walcott-family-euro-2012-racist (last accessed 31 March 2023); Rajeev Syal, "Ukraine's festering football racism", *The Guardian*, 1 June 2012, https://www.theguardian.com/world/2012/jun/01/euro-2012-ukraine-football-racism-sol-campbell (last accessed 31 March 2023).

24. See Benson and Lewis, "Brexit, British People of Colour in the EU-27 and everyday racism in Britain and Europe", pp. 2221–2222.

25. Jennifer Rankin, "The EU is too white—and Brexit likely to make it worse, MEPs and staff say", *The Guardian*, 29 August 2018, https://www.theguardian.com/world/2018/aug/29/eu-is-too-white-brexit-likely-to-make-it-worse (last accessed 31 March 2023); also "Brexit to have significant impact on racial diversity in the EU institutions", European Network Against Racism (ENAR), 31 January 2020, https://www.enar-eu.org/Brexit-to-have-significant-impact-on-racial-diversity-in-the-EU-institutions/ (last accessed 31 March 2023).

26. On the European Parliament, also see Johanna Kantola, Anna Elimäki, Barbara Gaweda, Cherry Miller, Petra Ahrens, and Valentine Berthet, "'It's Like Shouting to a Brick Wall': Normative Whiteness and Racism in the European Parliament", *American Political Science Review*, 19 July 2002, pp. 1–16.

27. The Race Relations Act 1965 outlawed racial discrimination in public places such as hotels and restaurants and created the Race Relations Board to adjudicate on complaints of racial discrimination. The Race Relations Act 1968 also outlawed racial discrimination in employment and housing. The Race Relations Act 1976 extended the definition of discrimination to include indirect discrimination. On the other hand, the first significant step to address racism taken by the EU itself, as opposed to member states, was the Racial Equality Directive of 2000. See "Council Directive 2000/43/EC of 29 June 2000 implementing the principle of equal treatment between persons irrespective of racial or ethnic origin", https://eur-lex.europa.eu/legal-content/EN/TXT/HTML/?uri=CELEX:32000L0043&from=EN (last accessed 31 March 2023). In 2020, the European Commission also published an Anti-Racism Action Plan. See "A Union of equality: EU anti-racism action plan 2020–2025", 18 September 2020, https://ec.europa.eu/info/sites/default/files/a_union_of_equality_eu_action_plan_against_racism_2020_-2025_en.pdf (last accessed 31 March 2023).

28. For a good overview of the economic and strategic stories, see Saunders, *Yes to Europe!*, chapter 1.

29. As Ian Sanjay Patel puts it: "After 1948, a non-white person born in colonial Kenya or Jamaica had enjoyed iden-

tical citizenship, on equal terms, to Winston Churchill." Ian Sanjay Patel, *We're Here Because You Were There. Immigration and the End of Empire* (London: Verso, 2021), p. 5. An interesting comparison here is with France, which undertook a similar reform of its empire around the same time. In 1946, as part of the reforms that created the Fourth Republic, the French Union was created, which abolished the previous status of colonial subject or *indigène*. Colonial citizens now had the same formal "quality of citizenship" as French citizens, including the right to settle in metropolitan France. See Frederick Cooper, *Citizenship between Empire and Nation: Remaking France and French Africa, 1945–1960* (Princeton: Princeton University Press, 2004).

30. On this coincidence see Patel, *We're Here Because You Were There*, p. 89.

31. Gaitskell speech to Labour Party Conference, 3 October 1962, cited in Saunders, *Yes to Europe!*, p. 259. The speech is best known for Gaitskell's claim that British accession to the EEC would mean "the end of a thousand years of history".

32. Saunders, "Brexit and Empire: 'Global Britain' and the Myth of Imperial Nostalgia", p. 5.

33. Ibid, pp. 10–13; Saunders, *Yes to Europe!*, p. 261.

34. On the economic and political consequences of this decision, see Thompson, "Inevitability and contingency: The political economy of Brexit", especially p. 438.

35. See Nicholas Watt and Patrick Wintour, "How immigration came to haunt Labour: the inside story", *The Guardian*, 24 March 2015, https://www.theguardian.com/news/2015/mar/24/how-immigration-came-to-haunt-labour-inside-story (last accessed 31 March 2023).

36. See Alan Travis, "Jamaicans dismayed by visa requirement", *The Guardian*, 9 January 2003, https://www.theguardian.com/uk/2003/jan/09/drugsandalcohol.immigrationpolicy (last accessed 31 March 2023).

37. See Amelia Hill, "'Hostile environment': the hardline Home Office policy tearing families apart", *The Guardian*, 28 November 2017, https://www.theguardian.com/uk-news/2017/nov/28/hostile-environment-the-hardline-home-office-policy-tearing-families-apart (last accessed 31 March 2023).

38. Office for National Statistics, "Long-term international migration, provisional: year ending June 2022", 24 November 2022, https://www.ons.gov.uk/peoplepopulationandcommunity/populationandmigration/internationalmigration/bulletins/longterminternationalmigrationprovisional/yearendingjune2022 (last accessed 31 March 2023).

39. "Britons welcome Hong Kongers as figures show UK issues over 110,000 BN(O) visas", British Future, 26 May 2022, https://www.britishfuture.org/britons-welcome-hong-kongers-as-figures-show-uk-issues-over-110000-bno-visas/ (last accessed 31 March 2023). The category of British Overseas citizen was introduced in the British Nationality Act 1981, introduced by the Thatcher government. It divided Citizens of the United Kingdom and Colonies into three new categories: British citizens; British Dependent Territories citizens; and British Overseas citizens. British Overseas Citizens did not have the automatic right to enter and live in the UK.

40. Gurminder Bhambra, "A Decolonial Project for Europe", *Journal of Common Market Studies*, Volume 60, Issue 2, 2002, pp. 229–244, here p. 230.

41. Ibid., p. 230.
42. Paul Gilroy, *After Empire. Melancholia or Convivial Culture?* (London: Routledge, 2004), p. 2.
43. Bhambra, "A Decolonial Project for Europe", p. 232.
44. Ibid., p. 231.
45. The exceptions to this would be countries that were ruled by several different European countries in succession. For example, Cameroon was ruled by Germany from 1884 until the end of World War I and then by France from 1919 until its independence in 1960. Thus, in this case, one could imagine a joint Franco-German restitutive project—though as far as I am aware no such project so far exists.
46. Bhambra, "A Decolonial Project for Europe", pp. 234–235.
47. József Böröcz and Mahua Sarkar write: "If seen as an organization that 'shares and pools' its member states' sovereignty, then the EU should also be recognized as sharing and pooling its member states' historical record of imperialism and colonial extraction from the rest of the world." József Böröcz and Mahua Sarkar, "What is the EU?", *International Sociology*, Volume 20, Issue 2, 2016, pp. 153–173, here p. 163.
48. Gilroy, *After Empire*, p. 98. Gilroy makes clear that, while his analysis focuses on the UK, it could also be applied to other western European countries with colonial histories, in particular Belgium, France, Italy, the Netherlands and Spain (p. 109).
49. Ibid., p. xi.
50. Gilroy is particularly critical of Robert Cooper, Blair's foreign policy adviser, who he describes as the "primary

spokesman" for the "new imperialism". Idem, *After Empire*, p. 173. Cooper went on to become Director-General for External and Politico-Military Affairs at the European Council and, after the creation of the European External Action Service in 2010, counsellor to High Representative Catherine Ashton. Elsewhere Gilroy suggested that revisionism about the British empire was accompanied by "the demand for its revival in a new form under the banner of the EU". Paul Gilroy, "Public Hearing: Debating Independence: Autonomy or Voluntary Colonialism?", Nuuk, Greenland, 22 April 2006, http://rethinking-nordic-colonialism.org/files/pdf/ACT2/ESSAYS/Gilroy.pdf (last accessed 31 March 2023). In short, Gilroy did not associate "postcolonial melancholia" with Eurosceptics.

51. On this point, also see Saunders, "Brexit and Empire: 'Global Britain' and the Myth of Imperial Nostalgia".

52. Gilroy, *After Empire*, p. 98.

53. Patel, *We're Here Because You Were There*, p. 6.

54. Gilroy, *After Empire*, p. 97.

55. The phrase was coined by A. Sivanandan. See Patel, *We're Here Because You Were There*.

# INDEX